Varieties
of Melancholy

Published in 2021 by The School of Life
First published in the USA in 2021
930 High Road, London, N12 9RT

Copyright © The School of Life 2021
Cover design by Marcia Mihotich
Typeset by Kerrypress
Printed in Latvia by Livonia

A proportion of this book has appeared online at www.theschooloflife.com/thebookoflife

Every effort has been made to contact the copyright holders of the material reproduced in this book. If any have been inadvertently overlooked, the publisher will be pleased to make restitution at the earliest opportunity.

The School of Life is a resource for helping us understand ourselves, for improving our relationships, our careers and our social lives – as well as for helping us find calm and get more out of our leisure hours. We do this through creating films, workshops, books, apps and gifts.

www.theschooloflife.com

ISBN 978-1-912891-60-3

10 9 8 7 6 5 4 3 2

Varieties
of Melancholy

The School of Life

Contents

Introduction

There are a great many ways of handling the unhappiness that inevitably comes with being human: we may rage or despair, we may scream or lament, we may sulk or cry. But there is perhaps no better way to confront the misery and incompleteness with which we are cursed than to settle on an emotion still too seldom discussed in the frenetic modern world: *melancholy*. Given the scale of the challenges we are up against, our goal shouldn't be to try to always be happy, but also – as importantly – to master ways of settling wisely and fruitfully into gentle sorrow. If we can refer to better and worse ways of suffering, then melancholy deserves to be celebrated as the optimal means of encountering the challenges of being alive.

It is key to determine from the outset what melancholy is *not*. It isn't bitterness. The melancholy person lacks any of the bitter one's latent optimism and, therefore, has no need to respond to disappointments with a resentful snarl. From an early age, they understood that most of life would be about pain, and structured their worldview accordingly. They aren't, of course, delighted by the suffering, the meanness and the hardship, but nor can they muster the confidence to believe that it was really meant to be any other way.

At the same time, melancholy is not anger. There was perhaps crossness somewhere at the outset, but it has long since dissipated into something far more mellow, more philosophical and more indulgent to the imperfection of everything. The melancholy greet what is terrible and frustrating with a weary 'of course': *of course* the partner wants to break up (just as we had finally grown used to them); *of course* the business is now closing; *of course* friends are deceptive; and *of course* the doctor is advising a referral to a specialist. These are exactly the sorts of horrific things that life has in store.

Nevertheless, the melancholy manage to resist paranoia. Bad things certainly happen, but not just specifically to them, and not for anything exceptional that they have done wrong: they are simply what befalls averagely flawed humans who have been around for a while. Everyone's luck runs out soon enough. The melancholy have factored in problems long ago.

Nor are the melancholic, for that matter, cynical: they aren't using their pessimism in a defensive way. They aren't compelled to denigrate everything in case they get hurt. They're still able to take pleasure in small things and to hope that one or two details might – every now and then – go right. They just know that nothing has been guaranteed.

Because melancholy is based on an awareness of the imperfection of everything, on the perennial gap between what should ideally be and what actually is, the melancholic are especially receptive to small islands of beauty and goodness. They can be deeply moved by flowers, by a tender moment in a children's book, by an unexpected gesture of kindness from someone they barely know, by sunlight falling on an old wall at dusk.

Where the melancholy suffer particularly is around demands to be cheerful. Office culture may be hard, and consumer society grating. Certain countries and cities seem more indulgent to the feeling than others. Melancholy is naturally at home in Hanoi and Bremen; it almost impossible to maintain in Los Angeles.

The aim of this book is to rehabilitate melancholy, to give it a more prominent and defined role and to make it easier to discuss. A community may be described as civilised to the extent to which it is prepared to countenance a prominent role for the emotion – to accept the idea of a melancholy love affair or a melancholy child, a melancholy holiday or a melancholy company culture. Certain ages – the 1400s in Italy, Edo-period Japan, late-19th-century Germany – have been more generously inclined to melancholy than others, granting the feeling prestige in a way that helped individuals to feel less persecuted or strange when it came to visit. The goal should be the creation of a more melancholically literate and accepting contemporary world.

What follows is a portrait of different kinds of melancholy. The reader is invited to think through their own examples, a task in which we are all potential experts. With melancholy returned to its rightful place, we will learn that the most sincere way to get to know someone is simply and directly to ask, with kindness and fellow-feeling: *and what makes you melancholy?*

(Top): Nicholas Hilliard, *Young Man Among Roses*, c. 1585–1595
(Bottom): Isaac Oliver, *Edward Herbert, 1st Baron Herbert of Cherbury*, 1613–1614

Intelligence
& Melancholy

Early on in the history of melancholy, the Greek philosopher Aristotle was said to have raised a question which can't help but sound a bit smug: *Why is it that so many of those who have become outstanding in philosophy, statesmanship, poetry or the arts have been melancholic?* As evidence of a link between melancholy and brilliance, Aristotle cited Plato, Socrates, Hercules and Ajax. The association stuck: in the Medieval period, melancholic people were said to have been born 'under the sign of Saturn', the then furthest known planet from the Earth, associated with cold and gloom – but also with the power to inspire extraordinary feats of imagination. There developed pride in being melancholic; such people could perhaps discern things that the more cheerful would miss.

Proud of their identities as ambassadors of sadness, young English aristocrats commissioned portraits of themselves in melancholy poses, wearing melancholy's characteristic colour (black) and gazing forlornly into the middle distance, sighing at an imperfection that they were smart enough not to deny.

In 1514, Albrecht Dürer depicted the figure of Melancholy as a dejected angel, surrounded by a range of neglected scientific and mathematical instruments. To one side of the angel he placed a polyhedron, one of the most complicated but technically perfect of geometric forms. The angel had fallen into dejection – the suggestion ran – at the contrast between her longing for rationality, precision, beauty and order, and the actual conditions of the world.

If we are to take Aristotle's question seriously, what is it that intelligent, melancholy people might notice that other, lesser minds may miss? To start a list: how insincere most social occasions are; the gap between what others say and what they mean; the bluster of politicians and corporations; the futility of all efforts to become famous or well thought of; the loneliness that dogs us even within the most intimate relationships; the disappointments of parenting; the compromises of friendship; the ugliness of cities; and the brevity of our own lives.

It would be far too simple to say that dark insights alone can make a person clever. In so far as we can fairly associate melancholy with intelligence, it is because the melancholy person skirts two characteristic errors of weaker minds: *rage* on the one hand, and *naïvety* on the other.

Like many an angry person, the melancholy soul knows that things are not as they should be, but, at the same time, they resist the temptation to respond to provocations with fury. They can seek justice, but they are all the while steadied by a ballast of realism. They will not suddenly be surprised by events and lash back at them with viciousness; they have known the broad dimensions of reality from the outset.

Albrecht Dürer,
Melencolia I, 1514

At the same time, melancholy positions a person ideally in relation to hope. The melancholic do not, like the naïve, imagine that they can have flawless lives. They don't play the lottery of romantic love or of professional success. They know the odds they would be beating with even a halfway-tolerable relationship and an only-sometimes-maddening job. But this doesn't have to mean that they can never smile or appreciate what is beautiful or tender. Arguably, it's their awareness of a fundamental darkness that lends them the energy to pay particular attention to the brighter moments that will at points streak across the pitch-black firmament. The melancholy can be intensely grateful and sometimes giddily joyful because they know grief so well – not because they have never suffered at all. They can be very keen to dance (badly) and to make a great deal out of a sunny day or a perfect meal. A child will laugh because something is funny; a melancholy adult will laugh with greater depth still, because they know how many things are so sad.

Being disappointed isn't any sort of intellectual achievement, and nor is being merry. The real feat of character is to keep one's fury in check even though one is a bit broken, and maintain hope even though much is self-evidently wretched. In so far as the melancholy person can lay claim to any form of superior intelligence, it isn't because they have read a lot of books or dress fetchingly in black. It's because they have succeeded at finding the best possible accommodation between the infinite disappointments and occasional wonders of life.

Pills
& Melancholy

Our culture is not only keen for us to find happiness, but it is also – on many occasions – distinctly intolerant of sorrowful moods. If we start to get down, it may seek to change the subject, recommend a thrilling film, encourage us to go skiing or show us something sugary or shiny. And if our state of mind were to remain gloomy, we would then be directed towards a psychiatrist who would play with our serotonin levels and aim to return us as quickly as possible to a state in which we would be able to join in with team sports, go to the office and honour our families and our duties to the state.

Psychiatric drugs have – in certain circumstances – offered major breakthroughs. The worry is not so much a society that wants to help us with our sadness as one that cannot, beneath the surface, abide that we should sometimes legitimately need to weep.

One of the routine assumptions made about babies is that they should always and invariably be up for a laugh. A certain kind of stranger who visits may, therefore, rigidly try to get a giggle out of them, by jangling keys, pulling extreme faces or starting a game of peekaboo. It seems a well meaning thing to do, but babies – like adults – often have weighty and serious things on their minds. They might, at a given moment, be missing the womb or wondering when the next feed might be, trying to work out what a leaf is or reflecting on how a button is held in place. A 'jollying' grown-up isn't simply happy; their particular sickness is that they cannot tolerate unhappiness in others, even an eight-month-old, because it threatens to highlight areas of grief that they have not processed or learnt to absorb in themselves. The baby's thoughtful face is at risk of evoking for them important people they have lost and regrets they have never come to terms with – and so the keys get jangled with ever greater ferocity.

A whole culture can, at scale, fall prey to a form of denied pain that passes itself off as good cheer. It may spend its time promoting vigour and triumph and leave aside how much in the life of everyone is also about loss, vulnerability and regret. In its eagerness to present a smiling face, a culture can fail to nurture rituals in which sadness can be mutualised, periods of nationwide mourning where a lot that is individually difficult can find collective expression and catharsis.

For example, birthdays shouldn't be framed – at the group level – purely as occasions for joy. They should be moments when what is incomplete can be confronted and sympathised with, in company. Mother's Day or Father's Day shouldn't be about sheer gratitude and delight; these days must also allow for ambivalence and anger (sometimes even fury), for only thereafter can expressions of love feel genuine. Likewise, family holidays should never be presented as moments of total festivity; they are times when we must be able to squabble, sulk and face up to what is radically imperfect about where we have come from. Rather than being squeamish about difficulties,

Zacharias Dolendo,
Saturn as Melancholy, 1595

an intelligent culture holds our hand through, and helps us to name, the sad regions of life.

By being too quick to prescribe pills for sadness, a culture is at risk of missing the necessary nature of melancholy. The melancholic doesn't need 'solutions' to their pain so much as an opportunity to share its details with people who are kind, non-judgemental and a little broken themselves. They want pain to be normalised; company around sadness is the chief 'solution' they need. Pills deny the melancholic the chance to address the isolation that lurks behind their sad moods.

By framing the melancholic as 'ill' and separating them from the rest of humanity, medical culture offers no lasting help to those it seeks to treat. Previous eras, though they might have been less medically gifted, were more psychologically canny. In a charming and emotionally intelligent fable, they allowed those subject to black moods to tell others that they had been born under the sign of Saturn and, because of the influence of this planet, would not always be up for joining in the singing, coming out to parties or chatting merrily. They weren't ill, and they weren't mad. They were just in a 'saturnine phase' and hoped to feel a bit better soon.

By avidly prescribing pills for sadness, we are hinting that sadness does not belong within a decent life. Far more than any pill, what we crave in our melancholy state is a warm-hearted community that understands the sorrows of life and is kind enough to allow us to sit with our feelings for as long as they may require to pass.

Loneliness
& Melancholy

It remains unhelpfully difficult to be able to admit that one is lonely. Unless one has recently been widowed or just moved to a new city, there are no respectable-sounding explanations for why someone would find themselves without a sufficient number of friends. The idea quickly forms that a person's loneliness must be explained by something diseased and troubling within their character. If they are lonely, it is because there are things in their nature that merit them being left alone.

Yet in reality, what makes someone feel lonely isn't usually that they have no one at all they can be with, but that they don't know a sufficient number of people who could *understand* the more sincere and quirk-filled parts of themselves. A warm body with whom to have a meal isn't hard to find; there is always someone with whom one might have a chat about the weather. But loneliness doesn't end the moment one is talking with someone. It ends when a companion is able to follow us as we reveal our pains and sorrows.

We stop feeling lonely when, at last, someone is there to hear how perplexing sex remains, how frightening death is, how much envy one feels, how many supposedly small things spark anxiety, how much one sometimes hates oneself, how weepy one can be, how much regret one has, how self-conscious one feels, how complex one's relationship to one's parents is, how much unexplored potential one has, how odd one is about different parts of one's body and how emotionally immature one remains. It's the capacity to be honest about these potentially embarrassing and little-spoken-of sides of human nature that connects us to others and finally brings our isolation to an end.

It's often said that we have built a lonely modern world. If this is so, it has nothing to do with our busy working schedules or gargantuan cities. It has to do with the fictions we tell ourselves about what we're like. We trade in brutally simplified caricatures, which leave out so much of our real natures – so much of the pain, confusion, wildness and extremity. We're lonely because we can't easily admit to other people what we know we're really like. We tell stories about what we've been up to lately that capture almost nothing of our truth – not because we are liars, but because we are ashamed of the gap between what we know of ourselves and what we are meant to be like. We're encouraged to present a cheerful, one-dimensional front from which everything awkward but essential has been planed off.

A first step towards ending loneliness would be to open the more secret doors of our minds by ourselves and step into the sad, angry, envious or self-hating rooms – turn on the lights and examine the contents without prudishness or denial, shame or guilt. Then, when we are next with someone else, we should risk discussing what we have found.

We are lonely because we have collectively been slow to accept that we are delightfully strange and unhinged. We should allow ourselves to reveal more of who we really are to those with the imagination to listen, and to allow them to bring their own weirdness to the table in turn. Our loneliness will end with honesty.

Achievement
& Melancholy

For most of our lives, we're hard at work. We're up till midnight in the library studying for a degree, we're learning a trade, building a business, writing a book. We have hardly a moment to ourselves. We don't even ask whether we are fulfilled; it's simply obvious that this is the bit that has to hurt. We fall asleep counting the weeks until we are finished with our work.

And then, finally, one day, slightly unexpectedly, the end arrives. Through slow and steady toil, we have achieved what we had been seeking for years: the book is done, the business is sold, the degree certificate is on the wall. People around us cheer and lay on a party; we might even take a holiday.

That is when, for those of us in the melancholy camp, unease is liable to descend. The beach is beautiful, the sky is flawless, there is a scent of lemon in the air from the orchard. We have nothing unpleasant to do. We can read, loll, play and dawdle. Why then are we so flat, disoriented and perhaps slightly tearful?

The mind works in deceptive ways. In order to generate the momentum required to prompt us to finish any task, our mind pretends that once the work is done, it will finally be content, and will accept reality as it is. It will cease its restless questions; it won't throw up random unease. It will be on our side.

However, our mind isn't in any way well suited to honouring such promises. It turns out to be vehemently opposed to, and endangered by, states of calm and relaxation. It can manage them, at best, for a day or so. And then, with cold rigour, it will be on its way again with worries and questions. It will ask us once more to account for ourselves, to ask what the point of us is, to doubt whether we are worthy or decent, to question what right we have to be.

Once hard work ends, there is nothing to stop our melancholy minds from leading us to the edge of an abyss we had been able to resist so long as our heads were down. We start to feel that no achievement will ever, in fact, be enough, that nothing we do can last or make a difference, that little is as good as it should be, that we are tainted by a basic guilt of being alive, that others around us are far more noble and able than we will ever be, that the blue sky is oppressive and frightening in its innocence – and that 'doing nothing' is the hardest thing we ever have to do.

Perhaps, deep down, the melancholy mind knows that the ultimate fate of the planet is to be absorbed by the Sun in 5 billion years and that everything is therefore vain, considered against a cosmological sense of time and space. We know that we are puny and irrelevant apparitions; we haven't been so much busy as protected from despair by deadlines, punishing schedules, work trips and late-night conference calls. A grossly inflated local sense of importance spared us a recognition of cosmic futility. But now, with the achievement secured, there is no defence left against existential terror. It is just us and, in the firmament above, the light of a billion billion dying stars. There are no more 8:30 a.m. meetings, no more revision notes and no more chapter deadlines to distract us from our metaphysical irrelevance.

We should be kinder to ourselves. Rather than putting ourselves through the infinitely demanding process of idling (as though a nervous, adrenaline-filled creature such as *Homo sapiens* could ever pull off such an implausible feat), we should be self-compassionate enough to keep setting ourselves one slightly irrelevant but well-camouflaged challenge after another – and do our very best to pretend that these matter inordinately and that there should be no sizeable gaps between them.

Our work exists to protect us from a brutal sense of despair and angst. We should ensure that we never stop having tasks to do – and never make that most reckless of moves, taking a long holiday, or – god forbid – embark on a truly foolhardy scheme, retiring.

Superfluity
& Melancholy

The world is hardly short of people. Quite why it needs yet another example, and why that example should be someone like us (with all our flaws, compulsions and mediocrities), is one of the conundrums that especially haunt those of us beset by melancholy. For these mournful souls, the first-order questions are never far away. Why are we here? What have we contributed? Are we worthy enough? Wouldn't it be better for us not to have been born?

It is these harsh enquiries that reverberate in melancholy minds and lends them their characteristically deep, sad and self-doubting expressions.

Perhaps the real puzzle isn't so much why some people doubt their existence as why certain others manage not to do so in any way. What lends these less sceptical characters their confidence that they have every right to be here? How do they manage to root their legs so firmly to the ground and why do they greet their face in the mirror with such a spirit of self-acceptance and vivid assurance? Why do they feast unquestioningly on the goodness of the Earth and never wonder if there hasn't, somewhere along the line, been some mistake?

At the root of the melancholic cast of mind there is likely to be a poignant psychological backstory in childhood: a lack of early love. No one who has been firmly and decisively wanted by those who put them on the Earth will ever doubt their essential right to be here. They will be permanently validated by the enthusiasm of their parents. These parents' songs and cuddles, laughter and care will strengthen them forever. They may suffer in all kinds of ways, and they won't be immune to a thousand pains and regrets that beset every human over the years, but they will never know the fundamental self-doubt that afflicts those whose parents didn't really want them. They will have a gift for speaking to themselves kindly and will look after their needs with tenderness during reversals. They will look benignly on their errors and forgive themselves in the way they were once forgiven. They will look after their own bodies and tuck themselves into bed in good time. They will suffer, but they won't hate themselves.

How different it is for the melancholic. In their childhood, it is likely no one was especially waiting for them to arrive; there was no emotional red carpet and no boundless admiration for their sweet toes and adorable eyelashes. No one was ready to lay down their life for their sake, or gaze at them with tender awe as they filled a bucket in the garden. A child doesn't have to be thrown into a dustbin to count as neglected. It may be regularly bathed and adequately dressed. There are subtler ways for an impression to form that one doesn't especially matter to anyone. The parents might have been very busy or the childminder often on the phone. Perhaps one's birth coincided with serious problems at the office. Or else a sibling got ill and there was only so much concern left over.

Or maybe one was a bit difficult, slow and shy and the parent looked elsewhere in embarrassment.

All this is enough to kick-start a worldview. It could, by itself, make one into a philosopher, someone who spends their life raising troubling structural questions, starting with the most urgent of them all: *why am I even here?*

It sounds insulting to have to believe that seventy-five years of gloom and self-questioning might have its origin in a lack of cuddles or bedtime stories before the age of four. Nevertheless, we would do well to accept the power of so-called 'small things' to determine the course of our lives – no less than we should humbly acknowledge the power of microscopic cell division to determine our biological fates.

Enthusiastic parental love is founded on a charming illusion: of course one doesn't – in the grander scheme – matter at all; of course one isn't especially cute or particularly worthy; naturally there isn't something fundamentally amazing about one's first steps or one's return home from school with a sticker for good behaviour in maths. Still, how pleasant and necessary for parents to weave around a child an aura of affection in order to inoculate them for life against stabs of self-doubt and self-hatred.

What gives the melancholy their clear-eyed intelligence – and often their dark humour – is that they have never had any illusory veil thrown over them. They have had to look at matters pretty clearly from the start. They haven't trusted teachers or many friends, and they have been suspicious of casual declarations of love. They've known how to be ironic and keep a keen eye out for pretension; such are the side benefits of not being too much on one's own side. The world is far more cruel, but also more interesting. And there will always be low moods when the whole thing doesn't seem worth it at all. That initial feeling of being unwanted persists forever. The great consolation is to know that we are not alone, that there is – blessedly – a silent community of people a bit like us, just waiting for art and friendship to bring us together.

Photos
& Melancholy

To those sensitive to melancholy, looking though an album of old photographs of ourselves is an especially poignant pastime.

A few pages in, there we are in a large colour portrait: a smiling five-year-old, pulling a gap-toothed smile, extremely proud of having just completed a drawing of a submarine and some very happy-looking fish. We're wearing our favourite dungarees and our hair is unusually long. We're also – if we can say it ourselves – very cute.

We may be moved at the sight of this little person, but also – probably – deeply saddened as well. How much of life's suffering this tiny thing didn't yet know! How much pain they still had ahead of them! They had no clue – that sunny afternoon in the garden of the old house, a few hours before it would have been time for a bowl of animal-shaped pasta and a strawberry yogurt for tea – what fate had in store. How little they could suspect of the divorce, the move to the smaller house, the bullying, the loneliness, the unrequited love, the guilty feelings around sex, the career mishaps, the trouble with their health, the realities of marriage, the financial anxiety, the romantic betrayals, the tetchiness, the ugliness of age, the persistent anxiety and fear and the troubles of child-raising ... to start a list that is in no way comprehensive or even especially ghastly (it can get much, much worse).

We're likely to realise, as we look at another photo of us attempting a cartwheel by a forest, that part of what keeps us going is the sheer fact of not knowing. We are kept alive by a brute biological appetite reliant on ignorance. But if we imagine being given the option of magically returning to being five again, knowing what we know now, we would most likely say a firm *no*. We aren't actively looking forward to death – we haven't got plans to end things prematurely – but we couldn't really bear to have our entire life again. Too many of our years have been spent in pain of one kind or another. There have been a few moments of fun and achievement, but, essentially, the score sheet has been too mixed to warrant another whole go. It's a melancholy realisation. Without our necessarily being fully aware of it, we don't find a great deal of what happens to us tolerable. There are too many days lost to anxiety and aggravation, self-doubt and alarm, loneliness and longing. We hate our lives more than we perhaps usually acknowledge. We want to go back and hug that little child for all the difficulties heading their way. We want to cry at their joyful innocence in a world which will make them suffer a lot.

Even worse, this retrospective glance can make us question the future. Right now, we still retain certain hopes. We may be trying to make a new relationship work or devoting a lot of effort to a professional project. If the past is any indication, though, within a decade (if we're lucky enough to have it), we'll be looking at a photo of ourselves today with some of the same emotions as those we now feel looking back on the five-year-old version of ourselves. We'll be seeing someone similarly naïve about what is to come, similarly innocent of difficulties, similarly overly excited given what is actually possible, given our nature and the conditions of life. Not only were we innocent in the past, but we are still fairly innocent about the future.

Many photos feel bittersweet; that is, not plain dreadful, but tinged with something difficult or shameful. Take a photo of us with our grandmother. We must be around nine. We loved spending time with her, helping her in her garden and laying out our toys in her front room. We also know that when adolescence came, we stopped going to see her. She seemed embarrassing and we imagined she couldn't understand much of what we were feeling, though we never tried to explain. When she died, we hadn't been to see her in over a year. We're still cut up about it to this day, and ever more so as time passes.

Then there's a shot of us with our first partner. We'd been lonely for so long and, finally, they'd taken us on. They were very kind to us – and obviously pretty young and fragile themselves. They look lovely, somewhere on the coast, with their hair blown about by a breeze, and their arm around us. We rented a little cabin and went for walks along the marshes. We rented some bikes the day before we left. Yet bitterness dogs us here too. After half a year or so, for reasons we still can't really understand, we told them it was over – and did so rather horribly. We were too embarrassed to be kind. We hurt them badly through fear. From the evidence on the internet, they seem pretty happily married now. They must hate us a lot. Sometimes, late at night, we wish we could call them up and tell them (though it sounds a bit mad) that we still love them.

Then there's a shot of us at university with a group of friends. It looks as though we're having fun. There's the guy whose name we can't even remember who was always putting on funny accents and once almost crashed his mother's car. There's the gloomy, clever physicist we loved talking to. How little we made of those precious years! We should have been more honest about what we actually felt. We should have dared to be a genuine friend to the others.

We start to realise how much of life has been less than we would have hoped. We aren't necessarily crying, but as we shut the photo album, we are one thing for sure: sad in the distinctive way we best call melancholy.

The Womb
& Melancholy

Let us return to young children. It seems appropriate that the world's most famous baby should have been melancholy. Though Jesus went on to have a very unusual and especially tragic destiny, there is a universal theme in his story, and that is what may touch us when we see him depicted as a child. Like all of us, he is sad – in part – because he has been forced to leave the womb.

This sounds odd, and it is meant to. After all, none of us ever remembers being in the womb; we don't go around with any active sense of nostalgia for our first home. The psychoanalyst Melanie Klein speculated that this was no coincidence: if we remembered the womb, then our sorrow for what we had been forced to give up and our dissatisfaction with our present circumstances might reach such a pitch, it would be too intense to bear. We have to forget what we once had as a price for having the courage to continue.

Nevertheless, it may be helpful to think of ourselves as still somewhere pining for the womb. By this, one means pining for a time when we were not so incomplete, a time when we didn't need to be afraid, when we didn't have apprehensions about

(Top): Workshop of Giovanni Bellini,
Madonna and Child. c. 1510
(Bottom): Sandro Botticelli, *Madonna and Child*, c. 1470

the future, when we were fused with someone else, when every one of our needs was magically catered for by blood pumping through a rubbery cable, whose stub remains on our front as a reminder of that original severance.

We may be nostalgic without knowing what for, nostalgic for a womb we have forgotten. There are moments of great closeness and comfort in adult life. Occasionally, we may be in a very tender person's arms; sometimes, someone cooks us a deeply tasty meal. But what can the most devoted lover offer us in terms of reassurance, or the most assiduous restaurant or hotel give us in terms of sensitivity to our needs, as compared with what was once on offer in our first home?

Given that we may be privately – and unconsciously – judging our adult experiences against the measure of very early perfection, it's no wonder if we often feel a bit dissatisfied and disconsolate. The biblical story of the expulsion from paradise is really a version of the story of our own birth. We all were once in a place where we didn't have to ask for anything, where nourishment came to us automatically and where we were in the hands of a kindly immense being.

No wonder many babies look a bit sad: they have lost so much. The religious are lucky, for they are offered a chance to return 'home' in the next life. For the secular melancholic, though, there is no pathway home. The lonely pilgrimage goes on forever. At least, if we are able to name the place we'd so love to return to, we may help ourselves to understand the scale (and the impossibility) of our desire. We should admit how much – despite all the advantages of adult life – we still really miss the womb.

Astronomy
& Melancholy

It is a mark of melancholy to be unable to buy into the status system. We melancholics know well enough what we're *meant* to care about: careers, money, the opinions of the community, the latest stories in the news, our identities in the eyes of others, where the economy is headed in the next decade. We know the purported significance, but we may also – in a private part of our minds – not care very much at all.

We're not merely cold or unfeeling. We've just ended up prone to seeing our species and our planet from a less human-centric perspective. Our eyes naturally settle not on what is directly in front of us but on how we might appear from 6 billion kilometres away. We're thinking not of what tomorrow will bring, but of how the present moment might seem in relation to the age of the Earth.

The natural place to take such feelings of disengagement is not – as society sometimes tells us – a psychotherapist's chair, but rather our planetariums and our departments of astronomy, our charts of the lunar surface and our galleries of images from the Voyager space probes. We may redeem our melancholic intuitions by studying the swirls of the Canis Major Dwarf

Pluto as viewed by the New Horizons
spacecraft, 2015

Galaxy, 236,000,000,000,000,000 kilometres from the Sun, or photographs of late afternoon on the Aeolis Palus plain of Mars. Astronomy is the true friend of the melancholy mind; NASA and the European Space Agency are its presiding deities.

Through our immersion in space, our alienated perspectives can be confirmed and returned to us with dignity. We are allowed to anchor our disengagement from the human drama to passing meteorites or the moons of Jupiter. Our loneliness can find a true home on the vast silent dune fields of Sputnik Planitia on the southern hemisphere of Pluto. Some of our sense of loss can be absorbed by the asteroid-pockmarked surface of the Moon. Our insignificance can be framed within the context of the 1,000,000,000,000,000,000,000 stars in the observable universe.

Planetariums may seem to be trying to show us the stars in order to equip us with the knowledge we'd require to become astronauts or physicists one day. In truth, they offer us a means by which to diminish ourselves in our own eyes; they are a tool with which to take the sting out of our nagging sense of unimportance and our frustration at our modest achievements and sense of isolation.

There can be good reasons for us to strive to live in the here and now. But there may be yet more powerful reasons to dwell for at least part of the day in the Proterozoic age of the Earth, between 2,500 million and 542 million years ago, when single-celled eukaryotes developed deep in the silence of giant, undisturbed oceans. We don't need to blame ourselves unduly if we feel at odds with our nagging fellow humans when we can establish imaginary companionship with some of the many wondrous forms in which life has manifested itself across planetary history, like the beguiling-looking *Psittacosaurus* parrot lizard who lived over 100 million years ago, or the dog-sized, tuft-tailed, two-legged *Chaoyangsaurus* who roamed the earth around 150 million years ago.

The best consolation for our sadness at how little ever works out is to cheer ourselves with the thought that the average stable lifespan of a star is only 10 billion years and that our Sun has already burnt for just under half of that. Soon enough, this middle-aged star's increased brightness will cause our oceans to evaporate, then it will run out of hydrogen and become a red giant star, expanding as far as Mars and absorbing the whole of our planet, including the atoms of everyone and everything that is annoying us so much today.

We should drown our tears in the ocean of suffering to which every living thing is subject. We should align our feelings of purposelessness with detailed news of the five mass extinctions to have befallen the planet. To every reversal, we should simply answer that there are 40 billion planetary systems at large in the universe. Before every anxiety-inducing date or speech, we should mutter to ourselves, like a talismanic prayer, that the Milky Way is 100,000 light years across and that the most distant known galaxy is GN-z11, 32 billion light years from the restaurant or conference centre.

The melancholy mind often suspects that everything may be a bit meaningless. Through astronomy, we can discover, in the most engaging and inadvertently life-affirming way possible, why and how it truly is exactly that.

Landscape
& Melancholy

As inhabitants of the modern world, we spend the major part of our lives in ugliness: under polluted leaden skies, among choked motorways, warehouses, freight depots and graffitied, shuttered shops. These environments continuously whisper to us that we are worthy of ridicule, and perhaps, that we should swiftly go home and hide under the bed clothes.

Then, on a few rare occasions, we end up somewhere extremely beautiful. We might have arrived at the old farmhouse late last night and only now, in the early morning, do we have a chance to see where we really are. We open the heavy, rusty shutters and take in the vista before us: soft rolling hills dotted with dark green cypress trees, fields of lavender and poppies, a limestone village on the horizon, a little church in the middle of an orchard, a stream below the house, bordered with weeping willows and clumps of bluebells … all of it emerging under flawless azure skies, as though none of us had ever been expelled from paradise and there was no such thing as death or pain. Someone forgot to tell this part of the world about human tragedy.

We feast on the scene and let the sun warm our face. It seems like the most exquisite setting we have ever seen or, perhaps, visited since we were children. And to think that only yesterday we were in our city apartment, looking at a rain-stained concrete wall opposite, the windows reverberating to the sounds of lorries idling at the lights below.

We should be happy, and in a way we are. Very happy. A farmer is leading some goats across the valley. A couple of children are cycling towards the village. But the beauty has also edged us into melancholy. We aren't sad because it isn't beautiful enough, but precisely because it is so beautiful – a kind of beauty we cannot bear to have been away from for so long and to have to live in exile from for most of our lives.

Beauty has served to highlight the ugliness that came before. We notice, in a way we couldn't yesterday, how much disappointment, violence, meanness and humiliation exist in our ordinary surroundings and routines. Thanks to the little limestone church (that we'll visit after breakfast) assembled by craftsmen around 1430, we're finally in a position to feel how much agony is latent in our hearts. We haven't been pain-free all this time. We've just been numb, holding in our sorrow because there was nowhere to discharge it, because there were no alternatives to it and nothing to remind us of the scale of our compromise.

The beauty of the landscape is like the very kind friend who, after a period of turmoil, puts a hand gently on ours and asks how we have been, and does so with such tenderness and intelligent concern that we surprise ourselves by bursting into tears that don't stop for a very long time. It can take kindness to make us realise how much suffering we were holding in. It can take beauty to make us realise how ugly things have become.

Of course, we want to move here. Somehow. We plot – as we have plotted so many times before, always in vain – how we might be able to throw in the job, sell the apartment and spend our remaining years in a little cottage. Every morning we would wake up to this and head out to fetch a newspaper and pastries. We also know it will never happen, and this is part of the mounting sadness. We have been reminded of a better way of living and, simultaneously, of our brute-headed inability to change our lives.

It isn't just the physical beauty that's touching us, it's everything that the beauty speaks of: confidence, clarity, ambition, virtue. Why have we drifted so far from all the values we hold dear? How have we allowed ourselves to lose sight of what matters? We are crying because this is where we belong and yet cannot find our way to. Our plane leaves the day after tomorrow.

We don't begin to know how to do such beauty justice. We are so trained in the arts of resignation, disappointment and surrender, we are such masters at defeat, that this offering embarrasses us. We take a stream of photographs, but they aren't really what we are after. We want to become somebody else, not just take photos of a valley.

That's why, on top of everything else, in one of the nicest places on Earth, we manage to be sad. Someone comes in and sees our eyes filled with tears. They wonder sweetly if they could fetch us anything to eat or a taxi to go sightseeing, but we are far stranger than we can begin to explain. We are crying tears of joy at a goodness we have missed out on; we are crying at the sight of a happiness we are emotionally too cowardly and inept to know how to make our own. We are crying because we don't want to be tourists; we want to be reborn.

Introversion
& Melancholy

The melancholy person will, almost by definition, probably also be an introvert. The modern world purports to respect both introverts and their opposites but, in practice, the action, the rewards and the glamour are all precisely designed to synchronise with the talents and sensibilities of those in the extroverted camp. To have any chance of seeming normal or achieving success, one must pull off a range of feats to which extroverts seem inherently well suited: impress strangers, attend conferences, make speeches, outshine competitors, manage people, join in with prevailing enthusiasms, reflect public opinion, socialise, travel a lot, go out often and date widely.

It can take a very long time before we realise that – however much we might hope for it to be otherwise – this is not, in fact, us at all. For our part, we happen to get very worried before going to parties; we have felt close to death before giving speeches; any kind of social occasion perturbs us heavily; we're left extremely jittery by encounters with news and social media; we start to feel sick if we haven't had the chance to sit on our own and process our thoughts for a few hours every day; new places (especially bedrooms) worry us hugely; we're very awkward about having to be responsible for anyone at work; and we are extremely wary of jolliness or demonstrations of group fervour of any kind. We don't actively hate hugs, but our bodies do stiffen when someone rushes forward to embrace us.

Conversely, we adore staying at home; we'd be quite happy spending a whole weekend (or even a few years) in our own company with some books and a laptop; we only properly like about three people in the world; we love exploring different rooms in our minds; we are reassured by friends who know how to confess their vulnerability and anxiety; we'd like never to have to go to a party again; we almost never complain that things are too quiet; and we love peaceful landscapes and uneventful days. We quite like flowers too.

All of this can bring intense suspicion to bear on us in the modern world. Why are we so timid? Why can't we sing along with everyone else? Why aren't we coming out to celebrate? We conclude that we are weird, and possibly ill, long before we can accept that we may just be very different.

To be a melancholic introvert is to be constantly impacted by the 'small things' that others may miss. What can make a party or a company meeting so exhausting for us is that we aren't merely expressing our thoughts and chatting. We'll wonder what everyone has made of what we've just said; we'll suspect that we have failed to understand an important dynamic; we'll be struck by a peculiar possible hostility from someone in the corner; we'll worry that our face has stuck in an unfortunate, gormless position. We are – when called upon – canny observers of the human comedy, but minute by minute, we are also exhaustingly self-conscious.

We long for connection, but relationships are a minefield, especially at the start. What do they really think of us? Are we allowed to express desire for them? Are they disgusted by us? No wonder if we prefer to stay at home with a book.

It sounds difficult, but an introverted life can also be a very grateful and rich one. We need so much less in order to have enough. We don't require noise and attention. We don't care where the giant party is. We just want to potter around in our boring clothes, chat to the few people we feel comfortable with, take walks and lie in the bath a lot. There can be so much in things when we let them resonate properly. How much we've already seen; how many journeys we've already been on; how much we've already read; what tumults we've already been through. We don't really need more. An introvert is someone prepared properly to take on board what an event or another person is – all that is daunting, powerful, resonant, beautiful or terrifying in experience.

Small children are natural introverts. When a stranger comes into the room, they instinctively turn to nestle in the bosom of their caregiver. And who can blame them, given how huge this new person is and how odd they sound and how much they want to go straight into a conversation, instead of spying warily for a while, as would feel so much more natural. These children also don't need too much stimulation from outside: playing with the lid of a cardboard box for a while is fascinating. They can have a lot of fun gazing at raindrops chasing each other down the window. They can lie on the floor in their bedroom and draw one version of a tree after another and not even notice it's already bath time. Also, they get exhausted easily: an hour at a lively birthday party and it's imperative to go straight home for a nap.

Recognising our melancholic introverted nature is not merely a piece of poetic self-knowledge. It belongs to our mental health – for failing to make the correct accommodation with our introversion is a fast route to overload and ensuing anxiety and paranoia. What we term a breakdown is often simply an introverted mind crying out for greater peace, rest, self-compassion and harmony. Experienced introverts, therefore, realise a need to push against the extroverted agenda. Their sanity relies on being able to cleave to the insular routines they require. We have at least got a vocabulary for explaining the structure of our personalities to others. The next step will be to learn how to honour it, and properly allow people to lead the quieter lives their temperaments deserve.

Sex
& Melancholy

Sex is a time, first and foremost, of great honesty. For most of our lives, we must dissemble and pretend, hide and compromise. We cannot reveal most of our true desires or wishes, but must proceed in terror that we might somewhere along the line cause grave offence or be thought peculiar and damnable.

But at last, in bed with someone we truly like and who likes us back with equal sincerity, we can let our guard down. There's no longer any need to pretend. This is as private and as intimate as it will ever get. One can finally do what one has – in a little corner of one's mind – been aching to do for so long: perhaps act in a totally submissive way or explore a ruthless, uncompromising side; dress in the clothes of another gender; or start uttering a litany of obscene and taboo phrases one would also like the partner to repeat carefully. What one chooses to be honest about will vary; the dream is always that one can land on something that feels especially significant and hitherto blocked by the rules of propriety.

The melancholy person approaches the honesty available in sex from a very particular angle. They are perhaps not especially interested in ropes or leather, in studs or fur collars. They may feel turned on by something altogether more distinctive: *crying*.

The most fundamental fact for the melancholic is that life is filled with unending pain, almost all of which they must hide. They cannot normally explain the scale of the distress they felt in childhood, the disappointments of adolescence, the fear and exhaustion of their careers, the frustrations and tetchiness of their relationships, the difficulties with their families, the existential terror they experience in the night, the unease they are hounded by at almost every moment … They are, somewhere in the background, carrying an intolerable sack of weariness and grief. Most of the time, they can't let on. They're good at smiling; they are accomplished people-pleasers. But the sadness doesn't go away. It lingers a millimetre below the emotional epidermis, looking out for occasions – it is often a poem or a photograph – when it might briefly emerge.

Yet now, in the bedroom with a sensitive soul, someone who is beautiful not because of what they look like but because of how they interpret and digest pain, what feels most urgent (alongside everything physical) isn't to whip or command, pull hair or shout, but to break down in tears. Tears at how hard it's been for so many decades, how brave one has had to seem, how many struggles one has swallowed. One is making love, and at the same time, weeping because no one has ever understood until now and because one has been endlessly humiliated, overlooked and terrified. And because it might, for a while, perhaps be over.

Ideally, the partner is doing much the same. They have likewise brought their grief to the bedroom – and both lovers are exchanging the most generous of gifts: an honest response to the shittiness of being alive. There is no longer a fear of vulnerability. Their physical nakedness is as nothing next to the emotional equivalent they're demonstrating. They are more honest than they have ever been and it's the most erotic moment of their lives.

The eroticism is key. The crying isn't just tender, it's actively a turn on; what we find erotic so often comprises an emotion we respect but have been cut off from for too long in ordinary life. The tears are exciting us because they are a symbol of long-lost honesty.

There are some very graceful and, no doubt, very attractive optimistic people, who could be exceptionally interesting lovers. A melancholy partner, however, will always have one big advantage over them: they know how to combine orgasms and tears.

It's because melancholics have, until now, been so shy about their orientations that the taste for sad sex has not been as prominent as it might have been. But as melancholy becomes more well known, more of us may start to discover a buried longing to be extremely happy with a lover because, in the close semi-darkness, we and they can finally give way to ecstatic sadness.

Post-Coitus
& Melancholy

If sex were as easy as our society sometimes suggests, we'd expect not to feel appreciably any different after, as opposed to before, the act. As it is, for many of us, what we go through immediately following orgasm isn't so much closeness or joy as a very particular kind of sadness, one all the more lonely and peculiar because it seems so hard to talk about without sounding ungrateful or mean. We may – in the aftermath of one of life's most pleasurable sensations – be thrown into intense post-coital melancholy.

As we lie in the semi-darkness, with our partner breathing gently beside us, sleep may elude us. Our minds may scour the inner landscape, refusing to let consciousness go. We may be alert and at the same time panicky, heavy and sad. How could something so joyful have precipitated such sorrow?

At the root of much post-coital melancholy is a shame as to how we have ended up in bed like this. Sex can stir up passions which are deeply at odds with our daily conduct and beliefs. In the name of sex, an otherwise sober and gentle person will beg to be tied up and flogged; a generally exceptionally loyal and careful person will violate every marital vow; in a noisy nightclub, an intelligent and thoughtful soul will spend hours chatting with a companion with whom they have no deeper connection.

The instant orgasm has occurred, the bad faith one has been involved in comes to light. In past ages, this would have been the moment to head to the church or temple. One would plunge oneself into holy water or say some ritual words of atonement to a grave-faced priest. We may scoff at such superstition, but these divine rituals existed for a reason: in their way, they recognised both the deep pull of the erotic and the contradictory claims of our higher minds. They were sympathetic to how strongly good people may long for dignity, fidelity and wisdom and yet simultaneously be drawn towards degeneracy and vice.

Our first experience of melancholic sexual guilt probably came in adolescence. As children, we might have been uncomplicatedly sweet; we could have told our mother everything; our favourite activity might have been horse-riding or playing with our trains. Then suddenly, we needed constantly to lock ourselves in the bathroom and think obsessively of certain scenarios. No sooner were we done than a darkness settled in on us which has – in many ways – never left us.

The melancholy and shame come especially to the fore after being with someone we don't particularly love, yet who might love us a lot. How could we, for the sake of a few moments of pleasure, act in such an amoral way? We might hope that we could turn to the kindly partner whose body we have lusted after and confess our inconsistency and lies and ask that they might absolve us of our transgression: how much we might feel for them if only they could understand that we didn't, despite what just happened, have any of the right feelings for them …

In post-coital exhaustion, we become aware of how much time we have squandered on sexual adventure. In the hours we have wasted scheming and plotting, we might have finished a script, written a business plan or sent in a university paper. We might have been looking after some small children who begged us to be back by bath time.

What we wish for more than anything is reassurance that we remain, despite everything, a sweet enough human being – just one with a complicated set of imperatives to juggle. We are melancholic after a certain kind of sex because we wish our lives could be simpler; we wish that sex didn't pull us in contrary directions; we wish that we could only ever love and desire the same person.

History
& Melancholy

Even though history is filled with stories of terrible events (wars, massacres, etc.), many people still manage to believe in progress. They trust that things broadly get better and that humanity has a bright future ahead of it.

However, melancholic people are not able to share this kind of optimism. When they look at the past, they see a degree of horror and pain they can't get over. In particular, they are conscious that many civilisations have existed that were brutally snuffed out – even though they would have had so much to give us.

The melancholy mind is drawn to moments when history appears to confirm a thesis familiar from individual life: that the best do not typically win, that the prizes often go to the undeserving and that a nobility of spirit can lead to an inability to summon up the strength to defeat an aggressive enemy. In the ruins of old civilisations, the melancholy observe a moral tale about the fate of virtue and honour in a rough world.

The melancholy may, for example, turn their thoughts to Britain at the start of the 5th century. There were symmetrically laid out towns in Verulamium (St Albans), Lindum (Lincoln) and Eboracum (York). There were limestone and marble baths at Aquae Sulis (Bath). Shops sold amphorae filled with olive oil from southern Spain and wine from Gaul; you could buy salted fish from Greece and preserved olives from Sicily. There was a high degree of order and some justice. And then in a few short years, four centuries of Roman rule in Britain came to a sorry end. The German tribes moved forward irresistibly across the Rhine, politics in Rome grew especially treacherous and the legions were abruptly summoned back to the centre. In villas around Britain, there was no time to make adequate preparations. Marauding bands of Saxons, Picts and Scotti looted and destroyed everything in sight. Much was laid to waste without any identifiable benefit to the invaders, perhaps simply to lessen their intimidation in the face of so much refinement. Anyone identified with Roman rule was at risk. In the chaos, fleeing families buried valuables in their gardens, in the vain hope that Rome might one day recover, and they would be able to return and restart their lives.

There were to be no hot baths again in Britain for twelve centuries and no more classical buildings for 1,235 years. People stopped using money and went back to bartering; the roads fell into disrepair; the towns emptied. Four-storey stone buildings with porticos and Corinthian columns gave way to thatched wooden huts.

One imagines how different it could have been if Roman rule had been able to unwind more gradually, with less rage and violence on the part of the conquerors. Had things worked out otherwise, people might have been reading Ovid and Seneca in Pons Aelius

(Newcastle) in the 6th century or taking hot baths under Doric arches in Durocornovium (Swindon) in the reign of King Offa of Mercia in the 8th century; there would have been no Dark Ages and no thousand-year wait for a Renaissance. Christianity might not have needed to impose itself with such savagery. In Rome, there would have been no impulse to smash up the Temple of Antoninus and Faustina in the middle of the Forum, and then crudely insert a church inside it and call it progress.

The melancholic feel sorry for all that has been lost. They can daydream about how different the Americas would have been if that fierce Spanish adventurer Hernán Cortés had been shipwrecked off Cuba in the late summer of 1519 and had not had the chance to butcher his way to the capital of the Aztec Empire, Tenochtitlan. A city of gardens and lakes, it was home to up to 400,000 inhabitants, the largest conurbation in the world at that time, and one of its most educated and decorous, filled with botanical gardens, arenas for playing *ullamaliztli* games, ordered residential districts and bustling markets selling slabs of dark chocolate, sweet cornbread, multicoloured parrots and the skins of jaguars. One wishes that this civilisation had managed to spend longer undisturbed under the rule of Emperor Moctezuma and his heirs, and so would have been able to acquire the horses, steel swords and biological immunity required to meet the West on its terms. Tenochtitlan might now be one of the great urban tapestries of the world, the Paris or Kyoto of Mesoamerica, its culture harmonised with modernity. It would be reachable by a fleet of advanced jetliners based at Etzalcualiztli International Airport that would have, painted on their tails (in a nostalgic throwback respected by modern Aztecs in the same way that an American might think of Abraham Lincoln), a rendering of Huitzilopochtli, father of the nation and god of war and the Sun.

One might likewise wish that the Nasrid dynasty that controlled the Emirate of Granada had not met such a definitive end in 1492; that Muhammad XII could have brokered a deal with Queen Isabella I of Castile and that this enlightened nation, administered from the intricately decorated chambers of the Alhambra Palace, could have continued to be a centre of learning, a home for multiple faiths and a centre for mathematics and poetry. One might no less wish that the Republic of Venice could have held out against the French in 1797 and, rather than becoming a quaint historical curiosity, could have remained a dynamic, independent city state, dedicated to business and the arts, the Singapore of the Adriatic. We can imagine its logo, the lion of St Mark, proudly emblazoned on the sides of its electric ships and online trading portals.

How much more interesting and less internally troubled the North American continent might have been if the European conquerors' westward progress had been stopped by treaty at the Rocky Mountains, after which travellers would still now be entering the territory of the Shoshone and the Paiutes, the Navajo and the Apache. What a useful counter to American exceptionalism it would have been if there were a low-rise Goshute metropolis near where Salt Lake City now stands; if, in place of San Francisco, there might be the Pomo Indian capital of Kunula (named after their sacred coyote); and if, all over the West, fast food outlets served dishes based on acorns, pumpkin and the flesh of cactuses.

The melancholy mind appreciates that it isn't the best, the cleverest or the most deserving who invariably win; it tends to be those most dedicated to slaughter, rule-bending and aggression – and (in many cases) those who have had the good fortune to live in a region with large tameable mammals to ride into battle and a 200-year head start in making gunpowder. Beneath a triumphalist narration of history, a far sadder idea emerges: that one can be noble and yet defeated. Also, and more hopefully, we may see that there can be such a thing as an honourable failure, a failure which demonstrates greater virtues of character than success, because it is founded on unusual reserves of honesty, imagination and tolerance. We have plenty to learn from some of the so-called 'losers' of history, not so much about realpolitik and power play, as about the sort of lives it might be truly civilised to lead.

Righteousness
& Melancholy

There is really only one question you ever need to direct at someone to work out whether or not they are a good person, and that is, with deliberate simplicity: *Do you think you are a good person?*

And to this there is only one acceptable answer. People who are genuinely good, people who know about kindness, patience, forgiveness, compromise, apology and gentleness always, always answer: *no.*

One cannot both be a good person and at the same time feel totally blameless and pure inside. Goodness is, one might say, the unique consequence of a keen awareness of one's capacity to be bad: that is, to be thoughtless, cruel and self-righteous. The price of being genuinely good has to be a constant suspicion that one might be a monster – combined with a fundamental hesitation about labelling anyone else monstrous.

Only properly bad people don't lie awake at night worrying about their characters. It has generally never occurred to the most difficult or dangerous people on the planet that they might be awful.

It is a grim paradox that the worst deeds that humans have ever been guilty of have been carried out by people with an easy conscience, people who felt they were definitely on the side of angels.

The melancholy have advanced knowledge of their impurity, and are experts in their own sinfulness. They can't forget how silly they have been at many moments and with what lack of thought they have treated others. This self-knowledge isn't fun, but it keeps them very honest.

One of history's most melancholy figures was also one of the kindest. In chapter 8 of the Gospel of Saint John, Jesus has recently come down from Galilee to Jerusalem when some Pharisees, members of a sect focused on precise adherence to Jewish tradition and law, present him with a married woman whom they have caught having sex with someone other than her husband. 'Teacher,' they ask him, 'this woman was caught in the very act of committing adultery. In our law, Moses commanded that such a woman must be stoned to death. Now what do you say?'

Jesus is being edged into a trap. Will he say that it is completely fine to have an affair (in other words, to condone something that one's society regards as sexually very wrong)? Or will the mild-mannered preacher of love and forgiveness turn out to be just as strict about legal matters as the Jewish authorities he liked to criticise? Jesus makes a deft move. He doesn't categorically deny the mob the right to stone the woman to death – but he adds one apparently small, but in practice epochal, caveat to this right. They can kill and destroy her to their hearts' content if, but only if, they can be absolutely sure that they have first satisfied one crucial criterion: they have never done anything wrong themselves.

Importantly, by this Jesus doesn't mean if they have never slept around outside of their marriage. He means if they have never done anything wrong at all, whatsoever, across any area of their lives. Only absolute moral purity grants us the right to be vicious, high-handed and unsparing towards transgressors. An important principle of ethics is being introduced: we are to be counted as properly innocent not when we are blameless in this or that area, but when we have done nothing wrong whatsoever, at any point and in any context. If we have, if we have slipped up in any field, even one very far removed from the crime at hand, then we are duty bound to stretch our powers of empathy, to strive to identify with the wrongdoer and to show them an advanced degree of mercy and charity. We may not have committed that particular crime, but we are implicated in sin more generally – and therefore must forgive. Jesus responds to the Pharisees with what have become immortal words: 'Let him who is without sin cast the first stone ...' The mob, understanding the rebuke, put down their projectiles and the terrified woman is spared.

The real target of this story is a perennial problem in the human soul: self-righteousness. Jesus's point is that the surest way to be kind is not to take pride in never having done a particular species of wrong. It lies in seeing that, inevitably, we too have been foolish and cruel at other moments, and in using that knowledge to foster compassion towards those whom it lies in our powers to 'stone'. A world in which we keep our own wrongs firmly in mind will be a very melancholy world; it will also be an exceptionally kind one.

Crushes
& Melancholy

We're in a queue at the supermarket; we're in the reading room at the library; we're in a corner seat of a train carriage; we're standing at the lights at a busy city intersection. Without warning, it happens: the immediate recognition, the sense of certainty, the start of the longing. Unobserved, we take in every detail: their ear lobes, the way their hair falls, the colour of their eyes, their wrists. We can imagine so much more: the stumbling but delighted first hello, the early dates, a walk in the park, the hesitant first touch of our hands, the initial tender kiss, a trip to the seaside, moving in, marriage, two sparky yet always adorable children. We sense the tenor of their soul: their kindness, sense of adventure, playfulness and good nature. We feel how much we would agree on other people, on politics, interior design, ways of travelling and of handling finances. We know they would share our joys and sympathise with our sorrows. Sometimes they would tease us or upbraid us a little, but we would know how right they were and how much we wanted to improve for them. We love the thoughtful way they are leaning slightly forward now and imagine lifting their hair and caressing the nape of their neck. We would so enjoy helping them with their difficulties, perhaps a troublesome parent or a worry at work, and would let them into our own struggles in turn. We worry that someone might be able to open our minds and see all we are thinking, but there is (as yet) no law against the silent work of our insane imaginations. We're keeping a very blank expression. If anything, we look almost emphatically disinterested in the world around us, even as, deep in our frontal lobe, we picture how we and our lover would together decorate the living room of our new apartment or log cabin. Then, as quickly as it began, the lights change, the train pulls into a station, they get up from the reading room desk, they swerve into the bagged salad aisle – and our hearts break.

There is paradox, and a high degree of madness, at play. Firstly, that we would do so little to approach a stranger whom we felt so intensely might be our destiny. Wouldn't it be normal to try to smile at them? Shouldn't we at least attempt to look at them directly? No, we would prefer to be thrown into a boiling cauldron. We dwell in permanent terror of bothering anyone. Hardwired into us is an advanced dread of causing the most remote inconvenience to another and, beneath this, a conviction of how unacceptable we essentially are. We love the stranger far too much to burden them with our fundamentally crooked selves.

Secondly, there is madness in spinning baroque tales around the outward form of an unknown being. We need to get to know someone slowly, refuse to project our longings onto a blank canvas and accept that love isn't an immoderate hope foisted onto the charming exterior of an unwitting innocent, but a process of slowly understanding a person's actual character with realism and downbeat patience. We understand that this habit of ours must spring from a very broken part of our nature: it must be a symptom of a fear of intimacy and a sign of an incapacity for true fulfilment. It's ultimately just a fancy way of staying very lonely.

But this is the true madness: though we know all this, and would always proclaim as much in sensible company, we don't – in our heart of hearts – believe any of it. When we can be honest with ourselves, we insist, against all the evidence, that the sensation we experienced on the train or in the supermarket, in the library or on the city street was not a delirious adolescent fantasy or an unreliable hormonal rush based on our traumatised early lives: it was love.

We know a lot about the mature forms of love that psychologists lecture us about; we may even have tried very hard to believe in them and put them into practice. We might be in a very sensible relationship already. What we experience in the face of the entrancing stranger, however, tells us that we remain, despite hours of emotional education, boundlessly romantic and entirely impervious to the call of logic or maturity. We know we should love only those we know well, only those who requite our desires and match our personality profiles. Yet we can't stop aching for the stranger we last saw on the platform. We're still thinking of them days later, and we would still now be able to evoke their facial features and personalities as we knew them to be from looking at the back of their shoes. We feel closer to love with these people – after a minute at the bus stop – than we do with many we've known for decades. With the others, we pretend. Here we are spontaneously and exquisitely overwhelmed.

We're too familiar with the demands of respectable life to let on. When people ask us where we've been, we'll report on the external movements, not the peregrinations of our demented minds. There are plenty of grave people lined up to tell us how silly all this is. It may well be that, and worse, but a resistant part of us wants to hold on to a more stubborn, beautiful and melancholy truth: that, despite everything, this crush belonged to the truest love we have ever known. We are members of a strange and shameful melancholy minority: those whose most profound and intense love affairs are with people they have never spoken to.

Parties
& Melancholy

Parties can be especially melancholic occasions. From the moment we arrive at most of them, we'll notice that intense efforts have been made to generate a welcoming and sociable atmosphere. Someone will have rigged up a sound system; there might be balloons bouncing around the ceiling; drinks may be brightly coloured. More significantly, some extremely well-meaning people will be keen for us to have a good time. As the evening unfolds, they might cheerfully come up to us and ask: *Are you well? Are you having fun?*

The intentions are moving, but the results can make us very sad. The vast majority of parties proceed with the view that what helps people to relax and feel content are displays of happiness, especially exuberant happiness. It is seeing another's good mood, hearing their stories of success and their joyful description of forward momentum, that will help us to tap into our own sources of delight and confidence.

It sounds logical, except that the truth of our psychology is stranger. What really breaks us out of our isolation is not to see others cheering, but to witness that the troubles that beset us – the shame, guilt, regret, despair, irritation and self-disgust

– are not merely personal curses, as we had suspected in the echo chambers of our fearful minds, but have counterparts in our fellow humans. It is the sorrows of others that confirm us in our gloom and help to raise our spirits.

With a new psychology of companionship in mind, we can start to imagine what a properly sociable party might look like. There might not be any loud, upbeat music, perhaps just a sorrowful Bach cello concerto or a Requiem Mass somewhere in the background. The host would invite us to share everything about our lives that was less than perfect and that society had censored in the world beyond. We would have the chance to reveal how dark some of our thoughts were, and the extent of our anxiety. Heading home after such an evening, we would be sincerely happy because we had finally been able to offload, and to hear from others, how much of life is about sadness.

It is easy to feel that one must be a misanthrope for not wanting to attend parties, but the opposite may in reality be true. We hate most parties because we are unusually keen for human connection, which we simply can't find at the level of depth we crave at the average gathering. We want to be alone not because we genuinely don't like company but because we like the real thing so much, and because the simulacrum of company on offer reminds us too powerfully of an isolation that breaks our hearts.

We are generally left standing at parties, surrounded by forty people, feeling more isolated than on the surface of Mercury, because the forty party-goers, who could have offered each other so much, are collectively trapped in an ideology of false jubilance. In a better future, we would learn how to throw those paradoxical-sounding occasions, melancholy parties. There would be no more jolliness on display. There would only be some unusually vulnerable and candid people sitting around, confessing how hard they found it to be human. That would be something to properly celebrate.

Splitting
& Melancholy

It is a characteristic temptation of the mind to declare things to be either very, very good or very, very bad. Nuance is not our species' strong point or natural resting place.

It was the singular achievement of the mid-20th-century child psychoanalyst Melanie Klein to trace this problem back to early childhood. For Klein, infants and small children are inveterate dividers of the world into opposing camps of the brilliant and the awful, and they act in this way from the moment they emerge and have their first feed at the breast. Klein proposed that a newborn has no clear idea, at the very start, that its mother is even a whole person. She is just, at the outset, a pair of breasts from which stems the source of all life and goodness. Sometimes, when a feed is going well, when the milk is flowing strongly and nourishingly, the breast is a source of delight and perfection, it is impeccable and superb, it is scrupulously *good*. But at other points, when it's hard to latch on to the nipple, when the milk is resistant, the frustration is intolerable. The baby deems the breast defective, vengeful, useless and definitively *bad*. And so, in a mental process that Klein famously termed 'splitting', the infant ends up dividing the mother into nothing less than a good and a bad breast.

Eventually the child develops a capacity for more integrated and complex thoughts. It makes an astonishing realisation: that the breasts actually belong to a full person. And more importantly, that this person happens to be (strangely) both good *and* bad, both helpful *and* frustrating, both gratifying *and* maddening. Furthermore, a lot of people seem to have this dual nature; they can be fun and interesting at one moment, then really very irritating at another. Far from reflecting some rare deficiency, this duality is part of every human being. The child begins to accept that they, too, are a mixture of the good and the bad, but that this is no reason to hate or give up on themselves. Life can be lived in shades of grey.

Klein was under no illusion about how easy these realisations might be to reach. She suggested that surrendering a black-and-white view is so hard for children that doing so will throw them into a period of melancholy thoughtfulness and contemplation that she called 'depressive realism'. In this mournful state, they will shed some of their uninhibited early liveliness. They begin to recognise that the world has nothing entirely pure to offer them – but then again, to compensate, that there are far fewer utterly horrible things as well. Mummy is very nice but also deeply annoying; Daddy is funny but sometimes infuriating. Nursery isn't constantly great, but it isn't hell either.

In the course of her therapeutic work, Klein realised that not every adult has managed to go through the stage of 'depressive realism'. A huge number of us are still stuck somewhere deep in the 'splitting' phase. That is, we continuously imagine that people and situations are completely pure and wonderful *or* appalling and detestable. Someone who doesn't agree with us politically is, for example, immediately a thorough villain: corrupt, hateful and deserving of total infamy. An ex-partner who has frustrated us must be a monster guilty of heinous behaviour and the worst motives. Someone who casts doubt on an idea of ours at the office is evidently entirely nefarious. The person we met on a dating site two and a half days ago is wholly beautiful and sensational to the core.

Klein's insight was to associate maturity with a rejection of all such divisive 'split' positions. To be a proper grown-up is to realise that there are no paragons or monsters, no deities or total reprobates. There are only people somewhere in the middle, trying to act well, making mistakes, striving to say sorry, hoping to do better – and always full of regrets and embarrassments.

Little babies are very sweet, but splitting is anything but. It can power some of the most noxious forms of vengefulness, intolerance and political oppression. There is an angry splitting toddler inside the general who orders the persecution of their enemies and inside the revolutionary who coldly has their victims eliminated. One of our greatest of all achievements is a melancholy and essential realisation: that everyone, not least ourselves, is a mixture of devil and angel and that, therefore, tolerance and forbearance are truly non-negotiable features of a bearable outlook.

Post-Religion
& Melancholy

The situation is simple enough if one believes in religion. Or doesn't believe. Where it starts to get complicated is if one firmly doesn't believe – never has and never will – but still profoundly wishes that one could; if one suffers from, as it were, a melancholic *nostalgia for religion*.

What might one 'miss' about religion? The list might include some of the following:

Mercy

We might long for a god who could forgive, who could be boundlessly merciful, who could understand that despite everything, deep inside, we did mean well. It's just that we messed up, we got carried away, we were stupid and we're so, so sorry. This god would look at us with a slightly severe and pained expression, but then would take us in their arms and say in a low, kind voice, 'I know you have tried. I know you are good. You will always have my love. I do not judge like the others.' We long for mercy personified.

Confession

The missing god would allow us to confess to everything: the terrible words we had said, the awful things we had done ... We wouldn't need to carry secrets and guilt forever. We could utter them to the god, kneel down on the ground, make a sign of atonement – and then be relieved of our burdens. We could start afresh and be reborn under loving eyes. We could have a second chance.

Prayer

At moments of special stress, we could lie in bed and pray, and the god would be there, somewhere in the darkened room, to listen. We would ask that our loved ones wouldn't have to suffer, that our career wouldn't be destroyed, that our relationship could be saved. Before a challenge, in the waiting room of the doctor's surgery, in the green room before a speech, we would ask that it could all be OK – and know that our god was there listening to our petitions and ready to bend reality for us.

Parents

We can be honest on this score: we all want divine versions of our parents. They would be solemn, dignified, patient and kind, always on hand to help and reassure – and, just as we might have hoped at the age of two or three, they would together know exactly what was going on and what needed to be done. If there was a problem, they would be on to it immediately. They would have the power to sort out all distress, and when we couldn't cope, we could go to them and weep and they would stroke our hair and promise that things would be fine eventually. When we were sick, they would tuck us up in bed, bring a boiled egg with soldiers, and after a story, give us a kiss on the forehead and leave the door ajar so there would always be a bit of light and we wouldn't have to be scared ever again.

Dignity

We may long for the seriousness and beauty of religion. In a house of prayer, the architecture directs the eye to eternity, the music summons the most serious parts of one's soul. There is an invitation to be wholly pure. In the temples of religion, we can at last leave behind the usual pettiness, squalor and our own more repulsive appetites. This is the true home from which we have been in exile.

A happy ending

More than anything, what we want from religion is an assurance of a happy ending, some sense that this won't all be a random, horrific nonsense that winds up with decline and meaningless death.

—

That all these longings are – at one level – entirely ridiculous and retrograde is no argument against them. We should allow ourselves to be nostalgic for ideas we know can't be true. That way we will be faithful to the workings of our own psychology, unlike atheists who not only declare that religion is nonsense but also deny the validity of any kind of wish for metaphysical tenderness or reassurance. We should allow ourselves to dwell in a state of post-religious melancholy, in which we can visit cathedrals, admire mosques, spend time in pagodas, follow services in synagogues and ache to believe – all the while bravely knowing that we are condemned to be forever alone, unreassured, ashamed and scared.

Sonnet 29
& Melancholy

When, in disgrace with fortune and men's eyes,
I all alone beweep my outcast state,
And trouble deaf heaven with my bootless cries,
And look upon myself and curse my fate,
Wishing me like to one more rich in hope,
Featured like him, like him with friends possessed,
Desiring this man's art and that man's scope,
With what I most enjoy contented least;
Yet in these thoughts myself almost despising,
Haply I think on thee, and then my state,
(Like to the lark at break of day arising
From sullen earth) sings hymns at heaven's gate;
    For thy sweet love remembered such wealth brings
    That then I scorn to change my state with kings.

Sonnet 29, written around 1592, finds William Shakespeare, then in his late twenties, in a highly melancholic state. He is worried about failure. He is contemplating a future in which he will be a social pariah, when mention of his name will be enough to provoke revulsion. He will be in agony, pondering his stupidity and bad luck. He will lament that he can't practise the job he most enjoys, and he will look around and feel desperation and envy at all those who remain so much more successful than he is and who still enjoy esteem and their good name.

It is, of course, a paradox that the most acclaimed writer in English literature should have worried so acutely about failure, and that he should have been so like us in fearing that he would one day – through a mixture of his own idiocy and unfortunate outside events – be a disgraced nobody. Then again, 'greatness' in literature doesn't come from living pompously among high-flown abstractions; great writers are ultimately simply those who know how to speak with special honesty about the panic and sadness of an ordinary life.

What had brought Shakespeare to this anxious, vigilant state? Why was he so afraid he was going to lose it all? Partly because he was not yet very well established. He'd only written *Richard III* and the three parts of *Henry VI*. In the coming years, he would write – in quick succession – *A Midsummer Night's Dream*, *The Merchant of Venice*, *As You Like It* and *Twelfth Night*. As yet, these would have been, at best, mere sketches in his mind. There was another problem. Shakespeare had a famous and very vicious enemy who was spreading rumours about him and seemed determined to bring him down. He was a fellow playwright called Robert Greene.

Greene loathed Shakespeare. He wrote an open letter warning that 'There is an upstart Crow, beautified with our feathers, that with his Tygers heart wrapt in a Players hide, supposes he is as well able to bombast out a blanke verse as the best of you.' He nicknamed him 'Shakescene', that is, a show-off and a popularising fool, and, to further rub in how untalented he was, a jack of all trades or 'Johannes Factotum'. In different circumstances, and with equal unfairness, we all have Robert Greenes around us. The world abounds in them, and they make life a good deal more terrifying and nastier than it should be.

The London theatre world was small, mean and very gossipy. This kind of review from a respected playwright was intended to damage and it would have done huge harm. One can imagine Shakespeare, still young and finding his feet in the capital, panicking at how bad the sniping was getting, worrying that such insults would never stop, knowing how many people had had a mean laugh at his expense, fearful that his good intentions would never surface and that he would forever be known as a cheap, unscrupulous idiot.

Furthermore, there was a bad plague in progress. The bubonic plague returned continually to England in the Elizabethan age. The year before Shakespeare's birth, an outbreak had killed 80,000. And now it was back. Between August 1592 and January 1593, 20,000 people died in the south-east of England, 15,000 of them in London. There was rioting in the streets and Queen Elizabeth moved out to Windsor Castle for safety. The government shut down all pubs and theatres for six months. Every actor and playwright was out of work. Not only was his name being trashed, but Shakespeare was also facing financial ruin.

How to bear the terror of failure? With Shakespeare as our guide, though the impulse may be to turn away from fear, what can calm us down is to sit with what scares us most. We should dare to investigate the terrifying scenario so as to drain it of its strangeness, and stop apprehending it only through the corners of our eyes in shame. Shakespeare openly meditates on what might happen: he pictures the worst that could unfold in order to see how it might be borne. He also renders himself cathartically vulnerable in the process; he makes no bones about his suffering, to us in the future and – one imagines – to the people more immediately around him. He is going to admit just how bad things are for him in order to break his isolation and sense of unacceptability. He will try to universalise what could otherwise feel like only a very personal and embarrassing affliction. He will dare to see if anyone else has ever suffered as he has, and hold out an imaginary hand of friendship to all his readers, as writers will.

Then comes the core of the consoling move. He recognises implicitly that what is driving his wish to be successful is the desire to be respected and liked. It is money and fame he is drawn to, but beneath these, there is another hunger: to be treated well and avoid humiliation. There is a quest for love hiding within the drive to be somebody. Once that idea is established, a deeply redemptive manoeuvre comes into view. We don't actually ever need the whole of society to love us. We don't have to have everyone on our side. Let the Robert Greenes of this world – and their many successors in newspapers, living rooms and social media down the ages – say their very worst and nastiest things and be done with them. All that one needs is the love of a few friends or even just one special person, and one can survive.

The love of a single sensitive and intelligent being can compensate us for the loss of love from the world. One can, as Shakespeare says, with such a gift, be in a better place than 'kings'. Popular success is an unreliable goal at the mercy of fickle fortune: there are so many jealous people and we are prone to make mistakes that they can use to bring us down. We must, therefore, try to find, and look forward to leaning on, the affection and regard of sympathetic companions. Others may be scoffing, or sneer every time our name comes up in conversation, but we will be secure; we will be somewhere far from the gossipy and plague-ridden city, living quietly with those who properly know us and for whom we won't need to do anything to deserve a place in their hearts.

Shakespeare's sonnet 29 has been prized for four centuries because it latches on with such sincerity to an anxiety that afflicts us all, and proposes a solution that we know must be correct. In the end, things may turn out all right: the plague might recede, business may pick up, the rumour mill may die down and leave us alone. Even if none of this happens, if it does all go wrong and we become a definitive byword for awfulness, then in our moments of high anxiety, especially late at night, we should know the fallback: a few generous, sincere, emotionally mature souls who know about forgiveness and kindness, sympathy and charity, who won't reduce us to one horrid nickname, who will love us with the complex regard that a parent might bestow on a child or a god on its creations. Love will redeem us. We may well fail, but we don't need to fear it will be hell – and so we can afford to approach challenges with a little more freedom and light-heartedness. The cleverest and most humane writer who ever lived knew as much and, in our panic, we should trust him.

Architecture
& Melancholy

A strange and rarely remarked upon feature of buildings is that they talk. They don't necessarily speak very loudly – sometimes it can just be a whisper – but if you go up to them and look at them properly, you can definitely hear them chatting.

Here's the Mauritshuis, a museum in the Hague completed in the classical style in the early 19th century:

I'm dignified and stately. I place great emphasis on manners. I aspire to be calm and rational, but I hope not to be cold. I like to leave space for sweetness and tenderness. How are you feeling?

Sometimes a building likes to chat about its view of the world more broadly. This is more from the Mauritshuis:

It's good to remember your ancestors because that helps to root you in time. We're just one tiny moment in an incredibly long story. So many challenges have been overcome. Keeping history in mind acts as a buffer against the agitation of the present. I've got some Ancient Greek and Roman relatives.

Let's listen to another, very different building, the Villa Savoye, built in a suburb of Paris by the Swiss architect Le Corbusier in 1931:

I'm from the future. I've had enough of tradition and the boring status quo. Recently, I journeyed in from another galaxy and settled down neatly in a pristine field. Stay with me and together we'll invent a new, better way of life.

Of course, not every building talks to us in an especially pleasant voice. Some of them can be shouty or impatient. They can be a bit like those people we meet who don't look us in the eye, don't register our mood and don't ask us anything about ourselves. In a suburb of Madrid, there's a large residential block put up by a team of Dutch architects that speaks very dramatically.

Hi kids, I'm not necessarily your age any more, but I'm certainly up for some fun! Do you like my new trainers? I'm so bored with convention. Let's shake it up a bit, out with the old, in with the wild! Dancing anyone?

The problem with buildings is that they have a great influence over our self-conception. Very often, we don't have a settled sense either of our value or of the stability and goodness of society. On a good day, things can feel tolerable; we have a measure of confidence in ourselves and faith in our fellow humans. But on others, we sense our mood dropping. We are anxious and guilty, and we don't feel very well disposed towards who we are; we wonder whether other people aren't simply cruel and out to get us.

Crucially for our state of mind, it's architecture that can help to push us either in a positive or a negative direction. It's what buildings happen to be speaking about that holds one of the great keys to our mental stability. In a street that speaks of forgiveness, gentleness and modesty, the world can feel benevolent; we can be at ease and ready to be kind to ourselves. If we're stuck for too long in other environments, the external world starts to amplify the worst lines of our inner world. There are streets that talk to us sharply about shame, about being a nobody, about our life being valueless, about only money and success counting: these are some of the forbidding messages that can be articulated by doors and windows, building volumes and cladding materials.

It shouldn't matter, but it tends to. Few of us are so impermeable to the voices of the streets that we don't get lastingly affected. That's why we ache for certain districts that can respect and like us – and are so scared of the remorseless negativity of others.

Those of us who are of a melancholic cast of mind should take special care with the buildings we spend time around. Their voices are likely to affect us particularly deeply. We are especially in need of messages that are going to support the more robust sides of our characters and keep our vulnerabilities at bay.

Most people, if they're ever in a position to commission a building, will tell architects about the number of rooms they need and the layouts they like. But if a key function of any work of architecture is to speak warmly to its vulnerable inhabitants, then in order to commission a house for a melancholic, one might ask an architect to work on a building that, when finished, would be able say some of the following:

I know life's often sad and difficult. I've been through a lot myself; I wasn't born yesterday. I'm not in flawless shape, but you can be bashed around and get through it and still retain your integrity. You don't need to be perfect to deserve to exist. You can be good enough. I'm cosy and strong. You've suffered a lot. I'm on your side.

Adolescence
& Melancholy

If there is any period of life in which a melancholic mood may be justified, then it is roughly between the ages of thirteen and twenty.

It is hard to imagine anyone going on to have a successful, or even somewhat contented, next six decades if they have not been the beneficiary of a good deal of agonising, sad introspection and intense dislocation in this period.

At the root of adolescent sorrow and rage is the recognition that life is hugely harder, more absurd and less fulfilling than we could ever hitherto have suspected – or had been led to suppose by kindly representatives of the adult world. The sentimental protection of childhood falls away and a range of searingly malevolent, but profoundly important, realisations strike.

For a start, we recognise that no one understands.

That isn't quite true, but, of course, the more complicated any human being is, the less likely they are to be easily and immediately understood. Therefore, as a child develops into an adult, the chances of those around them exactly sympathising with and swiftly grasping their inner condition necessarily decreases sharply.

The first response of the teenager is to think themselves uniquely cursed. The better eventual insight is that true connection with another person is possible, yet astonishingly rare. This leads the individual to a number of important moves. Firstly, to a heightened and more appropriate gratitude towards anyone who does understand. Secondly, to greater efforts to make themselves understood. The sullen grunts of early adolescence can give way to the enormous eloquence of the poetry, diaries and songs of later teenagehood. The most beautiful pieces of communication humanity has ever produced have largely been the work of people who couldn't find anyone in the vicinity they could talk to.

And, lastly, the sense that one is different from other people, though it may be searingly problematic at the time, represents a critical moment when a new generation starts to probe at and selectively improve upon the existing order. To be sixteen and find everything perfect as it is would be a terrifyingly sterile conclusion. A refusal to accept the folly, error and evil of the world is a precondition of later achievement. There really seems no alternative but to be miserable in mid-adolescence if we are to stand any chance of making a go of the rest of our lives.

Another key realisation of adolescence is that we hate our parents.

Yet it is truly an enormous tribute to the love and care of parents if their teenage children turn around and tell them at the top of their voices that they loathe them. It isn't a sign that something has gone wrong; it's evidence that the child knows they are loved. The really worrying teenagers aren't those who misbehave around their parents and take out their random misery upon them. It's those who are so worried about not being loved that they can't afford to put a foot wrong.

To develop proper trust in other human beings, it can be deeply important to be able to test a few examples, to tell them the very worst things we can think of, and then watch them stick around and forgive us. We have to have a few goes at breaking love to believe it can be solid.

And, of course, everyone's parents really are rather annoying in many ways, but that too is an important realisation. We would never leave home and become parents ourselves if we weren't, at some level, compensating for the problems, mistakes and vices we had first identified in our own parents at fourteen and a half.

Another source of teenage sorrow is how many big questions suddenly fill one's mind, not least: *what is the point of it all?* This questioning, too, is vital. The sorts of questions that adolescents raise tend to get a bad name, but that is more to do with how they answer them than with the questions themselves. What is the meaning of life? Why is there suffering? Why does capitalism not reward people more fairly? Adolescents are natural philosophers. The true endpoint of adolescence is not, as it's sometimes suggested, that we stop asking huge questions and get on with the day to day. It's that we acquire the resources and intelligence to build an entire life around the sort of big questions that first obsessed us at seventeen.

Lastly, and most poignantly, teenagers tend to hate themselves. They hate the way they look, how they speak, the way they come across. It feels like the opposite of being loved, but in fact, these isolated, self-hating moments are the start of love. These feelings are what will, one day, be at the bedrock of the ecstasy we'll feel in the presence of that rare partner who can accept and desire us back. Tenderness will mean nothing to us unless we first spent many nights alone crying ourselves to sleep.

Nature appears to have so arranged things that we really can't get to certain insights without suffering. The real distinction is between suffering with a purpose and suffering in vain. For all the horrors of adolescence, one of its glories is that the suffering it inflicts is largely securely rooted in some of the most crucial developments and realisations of adulthood. These fascinatingly miserable few years should be celebrated for offering us melancholy at its best.

Fifty
& Melancholy

Fifty is plainly and soberly the age of melancholy. Until then, rumours of decline could be warded off. In certain circumstances, we could even have been able to pass as youthful. With carefully chosen clothes and an up-to-date knowledge of music, we might not have stood out in a group of thirty-five-year-olds. If we had hazarded a self-regarding joke about advancing decrepitude, we might have been told to stop exaggerating and – as had been the intention all along – received reassurance and comfort. Now, the mention of our age prompts a visible wince from anyone more than five years below it. Fifty is no longer a jest or a cute dramatisation: this is the start of our old age.

An intimate knowledge of how fast it has gone since forty adds to the panic. A few more decades and there will be colostomy bags and wheelchairs. We may feel young inside, but our hands insist otherwise: they are the hands of old people. What we call a horrible picture of ourselves today will be one we will feel proud of in three years' time. 'Horrible pictures' are just a form of time travel; they are me-from-the-future sneaking in a visit.

By now, others will have started to die. Not the odd tragic one, as in our twenties, but constant cases. We start to scan obituaries.

Inevitably, there is a sexual component to our melancholy. We retreat in shame, knowing how sickening we must appear to so many. The thought of us as a sexual being fills most people with embarrassment. It feels like being desired by an elderly relative. It seems wholly against nature. We become, as a result of shame, highly formal, even distant. Younger people may think us unfriendly and verging on cold; we just want to be sure they know we haven't noticed them. They might declare us 'lovely' or 'sweet', the way one refers to a harmless pet.

We have, by this stage, accumulated a density of experience. Late at night, falling asleep, random images may come to mind – unbidden – of different sections of our lives: the desks at primary school, the first room at university, that little hotel in Paris, the trip to Los Angeles, the night in the Chinese restaurant, the light at dawn on the coast shortly after the birth. We have lived through so much that we may feel, at times, a thousand years old.

Luckily, by fifty, we are more capable of gratitude. We know for sure that it won't go on forever, and so we're prepared not to scoff at much that we might previously have ignored on the way to greater things. We've been through a sufficient number of panics and dramas to appreciate a quiet day. We've met enough people, and fear their complexity sufficiently, to be content on our own. Simultaneously, we are a bit less interested in ourselves. We know how much about us will never change and how much we have messed up. In compensation, odd periods of history start to fascinate us – other countries too. We wash away our egoism in a broader stream. Perhaps it doesn't matter quite so much what happens to our name and reputation. Success is a chimera; all it buys is momentary admiration, when what counts is connection and closeness, times when the usual bravery can be sloughed off, and we can admit how difficult it all is and how sad we are. Enough grandstanding and pretence; the only people who still interest us are the kind ones, who have suffered and know how to use their pain to connect with others.

We may grow increasingly moved by young children. Our own bigger offspring are brooding somewhere upstairs; they despise us now. But in the park, when we see a little one advancing happily towards its mother, in that drunken teetering way they have, we know exactly what it would feel like to pick them up; we remember their weight – that peculiar lightness that the human race has for a while – and long for the simplicity of this phase, when there wasn't quite so much resentment and we could be a hero for suggesting some dancing or an ice cream.

At fifty, we are at the top of the long slide down to death. For a few more years, we can stand upright, but soon enough our backs will stiffen, our knees will give way (they let out odd noises already) and it will be hard to put on socks. Still, we can't complain of an injustice or report the matter to the authorities. This is what happens to all of us. It's in the contract we signed at birth; it's not an outrage or a mistake, though that is exactly what it feels like.

The only way out is to wear our despair lightly, to turn it into a dark joke. It's too late to make big changes, but we can learn to carry our mediocrity with as much dignity as possible, to rediscover modesty and exit a range of situations we should no longer be in. We should settle into the mood most suited to our age; we should learn to live under the sign of Saturn, in a spirit of benign, ego-less melancholy.

Luxury
& Melancholy

There is an age, and a frame of mind, when we are strong enough to treat luxury with every bit of the disdain it deserves; when we know how to pour rightful scorn on its cost, its futility and most of all its vanity. When we are young and hopeful, we know that there is no need for an overpriced hotel when a hostel can just as well house our dreams. We understand the folly of those overblown seats at the front of the aircraft, whose occupants will touch down not a minute earlier. We have a future rich enough not to confuse paid-for kindness with love.

Then there comes an age, more sombre and melancholy in nature, when – if we have any possibility – we may find our Spartan honesty vibrate and start to crumble. We may invest in the roomier, more plushly carpeted section of the aircraft we'd once dismissed, and discover a happiness deeper than we had ever thought possible. In a plane, high above the Earth, we are looked after by a new friend who has troubled to learn our name and has hung our jacket in a closet with a wooden hanger! As we cross the Tropic of Cancer, and as down below in Madhya Pradesh, villages flicker by the light of paraffin lamps, we receive a tray on which an infinitely thoughtful and fascinating-sounding chef has laid out a small bread roll, a lobster tail salad, a filet mignon and what might be the sweetest hazelnut and chocolate cake we have ever tasted – and we may feel the onset of what could be tears at the beauty and kindness that surround us. It is, in its way, like being a child again, ministered to by a devoted parent during an especially vicious fever. Now that parent is dead, and we are far from being that little cute creature in elephant pyjamas that no one could hate and who had never done anything seriously wrong.

Or we may find ourselves in a foreign city and be unable to resist the call of an idiotically costly grand Belle Epoque hotel on the main square. After an hour of reading in our oversized tub, we may order room service and, soon after, receive a visit from another new friend, pushing a trolley that he steers to the foot of our immaculately turned down king-sized bed. The meal itself might not be anything wondrous, considered objectively – chicken schnitzel or a salmon tagliatelle – but what it symbolises is immense. They, our new family in the hotel, have kept things warm for us in a special heated recess under the table or covered it with a silver dome. Someone, an angel, has wondered if we might like flowers, and has inserted a tulip into a narrow glass vase, so as to cheer us as we eat. Someone else, a ministering deity, has worried about bread and provided a small but fascinatingly diverse selection (one with walnuts, another with olives, a third with garlic). Now kindly George from room service interrupts our daydream. He would like to know if we would prefer still or sparkling water. And should he pour balsamic or white wine vinegar over the tomato salad?

This sort of thing can end up mattering a lot (too much) because, in other areas of our lives, so much has gone wrong, for reasons that are at once complex but definitive. Our child no longer looks up when we greet them at breakfast; our spouse is filled with resentments. We seem to have lost most of our friends through neglect. There is so much that those close to us seem to hate us for. We are increasingly convinced of the utter meaninglessness and banality of our existence.

Oh, but here, in the luxury cabin or bedroom, it isn't – for a few hours – like this at all. Here there is only kindness and indulgence. It's all artificial, of course, engineered by monstrous sums of money, and would come to an end immediately if the credit card were declined (we'd be in prison within hours). Still, while the money flows, we can be in the presence of something astonishing and delightful: a portion of the kindness and consideration we crave, but hardly ever receive and know we don't deserve.

Money obviously cannot buy us what we truly want: the warm regard of those we live around. Yet it can, at points, at least buy us a few symbols of considerateness, and sometimes that might be the very best we can hope for, and that is realistically available to us, in our distinctly bathetic and radically imperfect lives. We may not always have the inner resources to find luxury the silly thing it actually is.

Sunday Evening
& Melancholy

It descends, normally, between around 5 p.m. and 7:30 p.m. and can be at its height at 6, especially when the weather is turning and the last of the daylight has burnished the sky a shade of crimson pink.

The Sunday evening melancholic feeling is ordinarily associated with work, and the prospect of going back to the office after a pleasant break. In truth, this doesn't quite cover the complexity of what is going on. It isn't just that we have some sort of work to do tomorrow that is dragging down our mood, but that we are going back to the wrong sort of work – even while we are in dire ignorance of what the right sort of work might actually be.

We all have inside us what we might term a true working self, a set of inclinations and capacities that long to exert themselves on the raw material of reality. We want to turn the vital bits of who we are into jobs and ensure that we can see ourselves reflected in the services and products we are involved in turning out. This is what we understand by the right job, and the need for one is as fundamental and as strong in us as the need to love. We can be as broken by a failure to find our professional destiny as we are by our inability to identify an intimate companion.

Feeling that we are in the wrong job, and that our true vocation lies undiscovered, is not a minor species of discomfort; it may be the central crisis of our lives.

We normally manage to keep this crisis at bay during the week. We are too busy and too driven by an immediate need for money. But it can come to trouble us on Sunday evenings. Like a ghost suspended between two worlds, the crisis has not been allowed either to live or to die, and so bangs at the door of consciousness, requiring resolution. We are sad because a part of us recognises that time is running out and that we are not presently doing what we should with what remains of our lives. The anguish of Sunday evening is our conscience trying to stir us inarticulately into making more of ourselves before time runs out.

Sunday evenings have a history. Until recently, the last hundred years or so, there was – for most of us – no question of our true selves ever finding expression in our work. We worked to survive and would be grateful for a minimal income. Such reduced expectations no longer hold. We know – because there are enough visible examples of people who have done so – that we could harness our sincere talents to the engines of commerce. We know that we don't have to be unhappy in this area, which adds a feeling of particular shame if we still are.

We should not be so hard on ourselves. We don't yet have the mechanisms in place to match all jobs to meaningful destinies. We can be both sure that we are not doing what we should, and wholly at sea about where our genuine purpose might lie.

The answer is patience and steadfast self-examination. We need some of the discipline of the detective, or an archaeologist reassembling the pieces of a smashed jar. We should not dismiss our angst blithely as 'the Sunday blues', to be assuaged with a drink and a film. We should see it as belonging to a confused, yet utterly central, search for a real self that has been buried under a need to please others and take care of short-term needs for status and money.

In other words, we should not keep our Sunday evening feelings simply for Sunday evenings. We should place these feelings at the centre of our lives and let them be the catalysts for a sustained exploration that continues throughout the week, over months and probably years, and that generates conversations with ourselves, with friends, with mentors and with professionals. Something very serious is going on when sadness and anxiety descend for a few hours on Sunday evenings. We aren't simply a bit bothered because we have to end two days of leisure; we're being made to suffer by a reminder to try to discover who we really are and to do justice to our talents before it is too late.

Agnes Martin,
Morning, 1965

Agnes Martin
& Melancholy

If there were to be a patron artist of melancholy, it might be the American abstract painter Agnes Martin. Over a long life (1912–2004), she produced hundreds of canvases, most of them 1.8 by 1.8 metres, showing not very much at all. From a distance, they can seem merely white or grey, though step nearer and you notice grid patterns hand drawn in pencil, beneath which run horizontal bands of colour, often a particularly subtle shade of grey, green, blue or pink. There is an invitation to slough off the normal superficiality of life and bathe in the void of emptiness; the effect is soothing and moving too. For reasons to be explored, we might want to start crying.

The works may appear simple, but their effects are anything but. 'Simplicity is never simple,' explained Martin, having studied Zen Buddhism for many years and learnt that encounters with little can be frightening, because they remind us of our own ultimate nothingness, which we otherwise escape through noise and frantic and purposeless activity. 'Simplicity is the hardest thing to achieve, from the standpoint of the East. I'm not sure the West even understands simplicity.'

In the little town of Taos, in the north central region of New Mexico, where Martin spent her last years, one can visit the Agnes Martin Chapel, an octagonal room, empty except for seven of her paintings and four steel cubes by her friend and fellow minimalist artist Donald Judd. Here we can sense how far we generally drift from what is important, how often we lose ourselves in meaningless chatter. The paintings bid us to throw aside our customary, relentless self-promotion. It is just us and the sound of our own heartbeat, the light coming in from an oculus above (across which a New Mexico cloud occasionally drifts), the patient work of thousands of hand-drawn grids repetitively punctuated by strips of the mildest hues of grey and pink – and the peace there would have been over the oceans when the Earth was first created.

We shouldn't suppose that Agnes Martin was herself anything like the peaceful canvases she turned out. When still a young woman, she was diagnosed as paranoid schizophrenic and suffered from repeated bouts of extreme depression. She would often hear voices in her head criticising her and urging her to take her own life. It could be hell inside her mind. But it is then all the more understandable that she might, as an artist, have felt compelled to produce some of the most serene works the world has ever known, and that she gained boundless relief from spending hours – decades in total – alone in a simple house on the edge of the New Mexico desert, listening to Bach and Beethoven, tracing grids on canvases and applying paint in colours that Zen Buddhism identifies with the renunciation of the ego and the alignment of the self with cosmic harmony.

The Agnes Martin Chapel, Taos,
New Mexico

If we are moved, it's not because our lives are themselves extremely serene. It's because, like the artist herself, we have for far too long been familiar with excessive noise. The canvases are like maps to a quiet destination we have lost sight of. We might point to them and say that this is where we actually, really belong. The paintings are how we could be if we sat with our own feelings a little longer, if we gave up using our clever minds to ward off sadness, if we made our peace with mystery.

Nowadays, by the typically perverse accidents of the art market, Agnes Martin's paintings cost as much as aeroplanes. Generally, they can only be seen in bustling public museums. In a better world, we'd all be able to have a few of our own. As it is, we can at least spend time with them in high-quality online versions and printed reproductions. They are sad pictures, in the best of ways. They know of our troubles; they understand how much we long for tenderness yet how rough everything has been day to day; they want us to have the simplicity of little children and the hearts of old, wise people who have stopped protesting and started to welcome experience. The titles that Martin gave her paintings indicate some of what she was getting at: *Loving Love*, *Gratitude*, *Friendship* and – best of all – *I Love the Whole World*, which implies the sort of love we experience not when everything has been hunky-dory, but when we have, after the longest time, come through from the other side of agony.

Agnes Martin, *I Love the Whole World*, 1993

Hokusai
& Melancholy

There are two ways of looking at Mount Fuji. As a geological phenomenon, it is classified as a stratovolcano, 3,700 metres high, 10,000 years old, which last exploded in 1707. It stands on the island of Honshū in central Japan, situated on the fault-line where the Amurian, Okhotsk and Philippine plates meet, with a mounting pressure inside its magma chamber of 1.6 megapascals and an average temperature at its summit of -5° Celsius.

But Mount Fuji is simultaneously a spiritual phenomenon, interpreted in both the Shinto and Zen Buddhist traditions as a conduit to, and guardian of, wisdom and enlightenment. There are temples and rituals in its honour. It is understood to have a meaning; it wants to tell us things. For Buddhism, humans are perpetually at risk of forgetting their true irrelevant position within the natural world. We overlook our powerlessness and unimportance in the universal order. This amnesia isn't a helpful illusion; it is responsible for much of our frustration, anger and vain self-assertion. We rage at events because we cannot see the necessities we are up against. So Buddhism regularly turns our attention to natural elements (rocks, rain showers, streams, giant cedar trees, the stars), because it sees these as helping us gracefully to come to terms with our subservience. We can be reminded that we have no alternative but to submit to nature's laws and that our freedom comes from adjusting our individual egos to what defies us. For Zen, Fuji is only the largest conveyor of a general truth, but it deserves special reverence because of the extraordinary elegance and simplicity with which it delivers its message. Its beauty, visible on a clear day when its cone is newly sprinkled with snow, makes it a little easier to accept that we will die, that nothing we achieve will matter and that we are as nothing next to the aeons of time to which the Earth has been witness.

The printmaker and artist Katsushika Hokusai was in his seventies and already famous across Japan when he hit on an idea that would immortalise his name. His project was to depict Fuji obliquely, in a series he called *Thirty-six Views of Mount Fuji*, published between 1830 and 1832.

We catch Fuji peeking out from behind a busy bridge over the Fuka river on its way out of Sumida; it's in the background as workers and travellers do business together in the Sundai district of Edo (Tokyo); it's there as some pilgrims have a picnic in the gardens of Kyoto's Ryōan-ji temple, and as a peasant leads a horse laden with saddlebags full of grass in Senju; it's watching as a half-naked craftsman makes a barrel in Owari province, and as workers fix the roof of the Mitsui department store in Edo; it's discreetly in the frame as some clam fishermen fill their baskets in Noboto Bay, and a group of pleasure-seekers have refreshments at a *hanami* (cherry blossom viewing) on Goten Hill near Shinagawa.

In some of the prints, the contrast between the puny defencelessness of vainglorious humans and the indifference of mighty nature is at a pitch. We feel pity and melancholy for what we are up against. In the tenth view in the series (overleaf), we see a group of travellers wending their way around rice paddies on the eastern sea route near Ejiri in Suruga province. It's autumn and a gust of wind has just blown. That's all that is needed to break our fragile hold on order; Hokusai's humans are at once thrown into chaos. They struggle to keep hold of their hats, their possessions fly into the paddy fields and someone's papers (it might be anything from the manuscript of a novel to some tax returns – though what it really stands for is human logic and presumption) are being carried off into oblivion, and might end up in an adjoining province or a nearby muddy ditch. This, Hokusai is telling us, is what humanity is: easily buffeted, one gust away from disaster, defenceless before nature, trying to work out what it all means on bits of paper that are as evanescent as fireflies.

(Overleaf): Katsushika Hokusai, *Ejiri in Suruga Province (Sunshū Ejiri)*, 10th image from the series *Thirty-six Views of Mount Fuji*, c. 1830–1832

In the eighth view, the sun is setting over Fuji; it will be dark in half an hour. A couple of hikers are ascending the steep Inume Pass while, a long way behind them, two traders are following with heavily laden horses. We can tell this latter pair are in trouble. Those horses won't make it up the pass in the darkness, and there's a strong risk someone will fall down a precipice. This may be the end of the road for the unfortunate traders. Even so, the wider mood is not mournful or panicked. Fuji is serene, as it always is, even when in its shadow, people are being buried, or dying of cancer, or imploring the heavens, or regretting their lives. Nature doesn't care one bit about us – which is both the origin of our damnation and, when we can accept the idea, a source of redemption.

Then there is the most famous view of all, the first in the series (see overleaf). Three fishing boats are out at sea off the coast of Kanagawa. They are the fast *oshiokuri-bune* boats, each powered by eight muscular rowers with two relief crew members. These craft catch fresh fish (typically, tuna, sea bass or flounder) for the marketplaces and restaurants of Edo, but today nature has other plans. It doesn't care about this evening's *makizushi* or the lives of thirty little people with families and dependents and hopes of their own. It has decided to send a giant wave, twelve metres high, to toss things about and remind humanity of who is in charge. We shudder for the fishermen's fates. This doesn't look like a picture of survival; it seems a prelude to a wake. Fuji looks on impassively, its tiny-seeming snow-capped peak impersonating the foaming sea closer by. We are pawns in the hands of forces that care nothing for us, and that will not mourn us for a moment when we are gone.

(Top): Katsushika Hokusai, *The Inume Pass in Kai Province (Kōshū Inume tōge)*, 8th image from the series *Thirty-six Views of Mount Fuji*, c. 1831–1832

(Overleaf)): Katsushika Hokusai, *Under the Wave off Kanagawa (Kanagawa oki nami ura)* or *The Great Wave*, 1st image from the series *Thirty-six Views of Mount Fuji*, c. 1830–1832

Hokusai could have chosen to anchor his melancholy meditations on human powerlessness to any number of natural phenomena: for example *Thirty-six Views of the Moon*, *Thirty-six Views of Drifting Clouds*, *Thirty-six Views of the Constellation Cassiopeia* (a dim speck in the night sky, 4,000 light years away). Against these, too, his genius could have shown up our exploits in all their absurdity: a couple squabbling, a writer finishing a book, a person weeping at their medical diagnosis, a lover pining for companionship.

We have to live knowing that most of what we do is, in a cosmic sense, ridiculous. Our lives are no more profound than that of an earthworm, and almost as fragile. In so far as we can ever recover a little meaning, it is by ceasing to worry so much about ourselves and identifying instead with planetary reality – even to the point where we might contemplate our own mortality with a degree of equanimity; by fully and generously appreciating our absurdity, and using it as a springboard to kindness, art and melancholy.

Travel
& Melancholy

Few moments in our lives are as melancholy as those in which we go travelling somewhere on our own. Imagine that it's late in the evening at a large airport somewhere in modernity. Most of the terminal is now empty; the few remaining departures are all for other continents. Most of us will be spending the night over an ocean turned silver by a brilliant moon. The waiting travellers are spread out across the terminal. Some are sleeping, most are checking messages, a few are looking pensively into the middle distance. Outside, maintenance crews are loading bags and fitting fuel hoses. Stacks of meals are being craned into galleys. Occasionally, a metallic voice reminds us to stay close to our luggage or announces that a plane is ready to board: Osaka, San Francisco, Beijing, Dubai. So many unforeseen, unknown places. The world is still, in its way, so large and unknown.

Through the plate glass windows, a roar of engines can be heard. Another giant ascends to the skies. Soon it will be our turn. Everyone here is a pilgrim, everyone seems lost – and this may offer us more of a sense of being understood than an environment that speaks in sentimental tones of settled community and family harmony. We are all misfit nomads here. No one belongs and therefore everyone can belong. We, who permanently feel like outsiders, may be nowhere more at home than in the lonely drift of a brightly lit airport at 11 p.m.

There can be a similar pleasing melancholy in a hotel room in a city where we know no one. For a whole evening, we may be on our own with the television, room service and a view onto 300 other similar windows across a courtyard. Our thoughts can feel newly expansive and free, released from the normal demands of home and its pressures to be coherent and predictable, knowable and tame. The unfamiliar furniture, the foreign soap operas on TV and the sounds of the city beyond release us to explore ideas we had resisted. From our bed, we can see a person in another room reading; above them, a couple appear to be arguing; in a third, a child is showing their teddy the view. We feel a rush of love for these people we will never meet, but with whom we are briefly sharing a slice of existence in a frightening anonymous concrete block on the edge of an ugly, wealthy city in a country we have no energy to understand. How much we might like to open up to them; how much secret sorrow and regret there will be; how worthy we all are of forgiveness and tenderness.

In anonymous places – airports, hotels, diners, train stations – we have an opportunity to meet disavowed sides of our characters: sadness, regret and loss. The bleakness all around is a relief from the false comforts of home. We don't have to pretend any longer. The environment supports us in our wish to own up to a sadness we may have hidden from for too long.

The fellow outsiders we encounter in these lonely places seem closer to offering us the true community we crave than the friends we should supposedly rely on.

There can be something almost beautiful about the ugliest kinds of travelling place: plasticised, brightly lit, garish, cheap. The lack of domesticity, the pitiless illumination and the anonymous furniture offer an alternative to the covert cruelty of ordinary good taste. It may be easier to give way to sadness here than in a cosy living room with wallpaper and framed photos.

We may feel most at home where there is no option to belong.

Misanthropy
& Melancholy

It's peculiar to think that a word like 'misanthropy' exists in our language: 'a dislike of humankind'. For a phenomenon to become a word, it needs a sufficient number of people to identify with it; it has to be an idea that we recognise in ourselves and others and then want to name and, in some cases, wear with pride.

That we have such a stark and straightforward word in so many languages suggests that, whatever our apparent allegiance to our species, it isn't very uncommon for a human being to look at who we are collectively – what we get up to, how we behave, how our thoughts run – and in the end want to give up. At the sight of our limitless violence, wickedness and folly, we may wish that humanity had never evolved. We may feel that *Homo sapiens* has ultimately proved an unending and undignified plague upon the Earth, whose reign should end without regret.

Misanthropy isn't bias or prejudice or snobbery. The misanthrope isn't singling out or prioritising any one group. They're treating everyone equally, even themselves. They've just reached the unfashionable view that we are a disgrace; that we don't deserve life. It is a supreme movement of the imagination:

to be human and yet to settle on the considered judgement that humans might be a cosmic error, a moral mistake.

What thoughts underpin the misanthrope's convictions? What is so appalling about us? A true list would be very, very long. A beginning might look like this:

• We are ineradicably violent. We keep justifying our recourse to brutality through an appeal to a higher goal (we are fighting for a little while for the sake of the motherland, for justice, for our god). Yet so regularly and gleefully do we erupt into cruelty that something more basic seems to be at play: we are violent because we have an ingrained taste for blood; we destroy because without a chance of a rampage, we would be *bored*; because it's, in the end, a lot of *fun* to fight.

• We are unavailingly vindictive. Someone does us wrong, but rather than being spurred on to a little more tolerance and humanity, our wounds charge us up to smite others back with even greater force the moment we have the chance. An eye for an eye is for weaklings; we'd rather just kill outright when it's our turn.

• We are immeasurably self-righteous. A part of our mind is constantly spinning a story about why it's right for us to do what we do, and erasing the slightest doubts as to actions or any possible need for self-examination or apology. It's always the others' fault; there's always a reason why we don't need to say sorry, and why we are victims rather than perpetrators. Placed end to end, our moments of guilt and atonement might amount to no more than half an hour across a lifetime. We are shameless.

•   We are fatefully inaccurate in who we punish. We are hurting, but the person who hurt us isn't in the room, or we can't get to them, so we redirect our rage onto the closest available defenceless target. We kick the dog on a grand, planetary scale.

•   We do eventually learn and improve. There's a higher chance of having good sense after some decades on the planet, but there are always newer, hungrier, more ferocious types coming on the scene, ready to refuel humanity's reserves of vehemence and savagery. We can't hold on to our insights; the wisdom painfully built up through wars, divorces and squabbles gets reliably erased every few years. We return to primal rage with every generation. Our knives get sharper and our weapons keener, but moral progress eludes us; the gap between our power and our acumen widens ineluctably. We're as dumb as we ever were.

•   We're entirely uncurious as to why people we dislike made mistakes. We gain far too much pleasure from calling them evil. We adore never for a moment having to imagine that they too might simply be worried or sad or operating under compulsions they regret. We thrive on a sense of our rectitude.

•   We are jealous of all the perceived advantages of others, but rather than admit to our feelings of inadequacy and impotence, we turn our sorrow into fervour. We attempt to destroy those who unwittingly humiliated us. We turn our feelings of smallness into sulphurous cruelty.

- We loathe compromise. We only want purity. We can't accept that something might be 'good enough' or that progress might come slowly. We'd rather burn the whole house down now than patiently fix a wall.

- We find gratitude intolerably boring; we're sick of having to appreciate what we have. Grievance is so much more interesting.

- We can't laugh because we don't, despite everything, find ourselves ridiculous. We hire professional comedians, as though finding ourselves stupid were a possibility someone else had to explore for us.

- We're obsessed by justice, and we think so little of kindness. Justice means giving people what they are owed; kindness – a far more important quality – means giving someone something they're not owed, but desperately need anyway. It means knowing how to be merciful.

Melancholic misanthropists love people, of course – or they did, once upon a time. What high hopes one has to have started with in order to end up feeling so sad at the state of our species. How much one would need to love humanity in order to conclude that we're a cosmic error. Melancholic misanthropists aren't mean; they're just casting around for a few solid reasons to keep faith with the human experiment. And, for the moment at least, they're struggling.

Extinction
& Melancholy

One day, if human civilisation ever wipes itself out, aliens or one of our successors will cast an eye on our ruined planet and ask themselves whatever happened to *Homo sapiens*. Their answer might look a little like this.

The root cause won't be the specific catastrophe, conflict or devastation that eradicates us; the problem will begin with the architecture of the human brain.

This tool will be remembered for being, in part, deeply impressive, containing 100 billion neurons capable of extraordinary computations and combinations. As aliens will note, a particular part of the mind where our most dazzling thoughts unfolded was known to neuroscientists as the neocortex – a part that was many times larger in humans than in any other species. This is what helped this hugely clever ape to produce *The Magic Flute*, *Anna Karenina*, Concorde and civilisations.

However, our alien friends will also note that the human mind contained another component, very influential but far less impressive, known as the reptilian brain. This is an aggressive, lustful, impulsive section of machinery, with a great deal more in common with what might be found in a hyena or a small rodent.

Because of this reptilian brain, *Homo sapiens* ended up with three grave problems:

1. Tribalism. Humans were always on the verge of developing violent hatreds of foreigners and manifested strong ongoing tendencies to slaughter strangers in vast numbers. They could never reliably see the humanity in all members of their own kind.

2. *Homo sapiens* was fatefully prone to short-term thinking. Even when confronted by data, the species could only imagine the near-term future, a few years at best, viewing the long-term as a chimerical and unreal state. Humans' immediate impulses were left uncontained and worked to destroy their individual and collective future.

3. *Homo sapiens* had an especially keen fondness for wishful thinking. Though capable of immense intellectual achievement, the human mind hated to reflect on itself; it couldn't bear to submit its ideas to rational scrutiny, and preferred to act rather than think, and daydream rather than plan. Having invented the scientific method, it preferred – in most cases – not to use it. It had a narcotic desire for distraction and fantasy. It didn't want to know itself.

For many generations, these three flaws were more or less endured. Certain institutions were invented to attenuate them: the law, sound government, education, philosophy, science. It worked, sort of. Humans kept wiping out swathes of their fellows, but they didn't scupper the species as a whole. What caused the ultimate destruction was the increasing, yet untrammelled, power of the neocortex. This mighty tool eventually managed to capture fire, contain the elements and give *Homo sapiens* a godlike power over the planet – while the animal overall still operated with reflexes akin to those of a hyena. The cost of the species' mistakes grew ever larger, and its powers became uncontained while its wisdom remained intermittent and fragile. Eventually, its might outpaced its capacity for self-control; it became a nuclear-armed rodent.

There was one thing that might have saved humanity: love. Three varieties of it in particular:

1. Love of the stranger: the capacity to see the other as like ourselves and worthy of the same mercy and charity.

2. Love of the unborn: the concern for those who do not yet exist and whom we will never know, but whose lives we are shaping in the selfish present.

3. Love of the truth: the strength to resist illusion and lies and square up to uncomfortable facts of all kinds.

We don't need to be aliens of the future to understand all this. We can see the disaster scenario only too well right now. The fate of civilisation lies ultimately not in the law courts, at the ballot box or in the corridors of governments. It lies in our ability to master the most short-term, selfish and violent of our impulses active in the dense folds of organic matter between our ears; it lies in learning how to try relentlessly to compensate for the flawed architecture of our minds.

America
& Melancholy

Most countries know deep in their bones that life is – for the most part – a painful and unsatisfactory business. Misery is the norm; one is born to suffer; the rewards may come, if at all, in another life. To suggest that happiness might be a right and to inscribe this ambition explicitly in one's founding document is one part, and perhaps the most significant, of what has from the outset rendered the United States an exception among nations.

No visitor will fail to note the expressions of this constitutional hedonism. The greetings are effusive, the smiles acute. Gigantic billboards express the national catechism along the highways, and the radio voices are frenziedly jubilant. Everyone is on an upwards path. Jerusalem is not a mythic city in the next world; it is to be built right here, with these hands, on this hill.

Artists of the American republic have never found it hard to create an ironic effect simply by placing, and exploring, the lives of real people against the backdrop of this self-proclaimed earthly Jerusalem. Here is a 'regular' upstanding family man at Disneyland's Enchanted Castle, texting his lover and plotting his escape. Here is a fractious couple moving towards divorce at the Paradise Resort in Malibu. Here is the ostracised prom queen, weeping by her stretch limousine. And here is an enthusiastic RV salesman, who will in a few hours shoot himself with a .45 in the parking lot of the Sunshine Motel. In far more accomplished ways, in half a dozen art forms, we've been here many, many times before.

What is being mocked is how hard the surrounding culture has made it for people to reconcile themselves to their own reality. Self-acceptance can feel impossible when perfection is meant to be the norm. What chances does one have to cry without shame in Happy, Texas ('the town without a frown')? Grief is left to be viewed as a damning personal deficiency rather than what it might otherwise and more consolingly be known as: an inevitable outcome of existence in a disenchanted, venal world.

The American misery that does exist is quickly medicalised and, if possible, expunged chemically. Or else, when someone can be blamed for it, there may be a lawsuit. What is intolerable is that sorrow should be interpreted as a general rule, which might not be immediately cured or neatly pinned to a personal failing. America is a very difficult place in which to admit to melancholy. The feeling isn't merely evidence of an individual loss of spirit; it's an affront to national destiny.

Psychology teaches us that manic happiness is frequently a symptom of a pain that cannot be faced. A smile has to become permanent in order that an underlying sorrow can never be felt. By extension, America may be smiling very hard not because it is genuinely carefree, but because there are a few things it simply cannot bear to mourn.

The impossible promise of
eternal, unbroken happiness.
(Top): Coca-Cola billboard,
Los Angeles, USA, c. 1980
(Bottom): 'Welcome to Happy,
The Town Without A Frown',
Texas, USA

It is telling that there are two groups within the United States who have never found it hard to own up to sadness. At the centre of Native American history is the Trail of Tears, a memory of the forcible mass removal of the Cherokees – against the explicit promises of earlier leaders in Washington – from their lands east of the Mississippi to what is now Oklahoma. There are, unsurprisingly, few happy faces staring back at us from 19th-century Native American portraits. In many communities, Thanksgiving is plainly known as the National Day of Mourning.

African Americans have passed through a comparably bleak experience of the republic. Not for nothing has one of their major cultural contributions to the history of music been known, quite simply, as the 'blues'. No wonder the smiles in the dominant culture have often had to be so bright to cover up so many tears.

All countries have their horrors and all peoples their sources of guilt. There can be no purity and no unalloyed pride. The more a nation is able to accept how much it has, across its history, been involved in pain, the more it can come to a natural and mature relationship to darkness. It won't need to smile so perfectly and so avidly, like someone who is in flight from something they cannot mourn; it can learn more easily to walk, and take ownership of, its own trail of tears.

AGE 82 ELIZABETH (BROWN) STEPHENS TAKEN 1903

(Top): Elizabeth 'Betsy' Brown Stephens, 1903, a Cherokee Indian who walked the Trail of Tears in 1838
(Bottom): The Trail of Tears memorial monument, New Echota, Georgia, which honours the 4,000 Cherokees who died on the Trail of Tears

Animals
& Melancholy

There are, in aggregate, far more of them than there are of us. We're a mere 7.5 billion, while there are 19 billion chickens, 1 billion sheep, 1 billion pigs and 1.5 billion cows.

They certainly cannot be happy, yet they can never complain. They are structurally among the most melancholic living things on the planet. To understand the essence of sadness, we don't need to read poetry by a tubercular 19th-century poet or the analyses of a mid-20th-century existential philosopher. We need only spend a few minutes gazing into the eyes of a Black Angus cow, who has had two summers on the Earth and is now a few days away from slaughter.

It would be stretching credulity to say that they could understand exactly what was coming for them. We can hazard that they might feel that something was awry; that the system into which they were born was too systematised and structured to be wholly honest; that there was something suspicious in those calorie-rich meals they were constantly being fed, with scarcely time to pause and ruminate; that there was a worrying brutality in the manner of the men herding them from steel enclosure to steel enclosure or jabbing them with vitamins and hormones; that those repeated disappearances and the bellowing near the trucks might one day catch up with them.

It is often said that we wouldn't eat meat if we could see inside an abattoir. But our consciences might be stirred far earlier and less dramatically, simply if we spent two minutes forcing ourselves to look into the eyes of a condemned cow at the edge of a field. What is most humbling is their passivity and readiness to be kind. One might fear that they would come to their senses and attack. We would deserve it if they kicked us to death. Instead, if we place a little grass on our palm, they will pull what passes for a smile and let their large fleshy tongue whip the snack up into their mouths. They let us stroke their noses and caress their flanks – which will soon be hanging from a fast-moving hook in a refrigerated chamber covered in discarded hooves, tails, faeces expelled in a panic and splatterings of brown-red blood.

It's as though they know, as they stare back at us. They know our cheap desires, our cover-ups, our paltry excuses, our absurd claims to enlightenment and goodness, how we have done nothing but hoodwink them since it all began in central Anatolia 10,000 years ago. At least at the start, their lives were expensive and precious enough to be revered; some self-righteous human might have written a poem or organised a festival the day they were slaughtered. It was ridiculous, but better than being hung upside down and shot coldly in the head along with another fifty of the herd you grew up with, and then winding up with bits of your rib half eaten on a ketchup-smeared plate in a diner somewhere off the motorway, and your skin used to cover the sofa.

They aren't making us feel guilty; we feel very guilty anyway. We know they are far more like us than would be comfortable; they are – in a cosmos mostly filled with inert gases and rock – fellow complex cellular life forms. They're almost our siblings. We can only go through with it by constantly telling ourselves the many ways in which they are not like us: they can't speak in finished sentences, they can't think, they can't do maths, they haven't read Plutarch … therefore what we are doing is fine, they probably don't much like life to begin with. They're almost willing to turn themselves into supper, as a way of saying thank you for all that feed. This must have been the kind of reasoning the Spanish missionaries used as they killed their way around South America.

Perhaps it is too easy, as a vegan or vegetarian, to believe in one's purity. The anguished, reflexive meat-eater is maybe more properly on the horns of the human dilemma: that our lives are always at a fundamental level bought at the expense of something else; that we exist because lots of other living things died for us; that we are an incurably rapacious species; that we have no right to be anything but sickened by ourselves on every occasion on which we contemplate who we really are.

The only compensation for the cattle on their way to be shot lies in the laws of biology. The life cycle will catch up with every murderer (us) soon enough. We, in turn, will be nibbled through by starving, unguilty maggots and worms; bits of us will soon be another being's lunch and no one will, or should, cry.

Jan Brueghel (the Younger),
Paradise, c. 1650

Tahiti
& Melancholy

We have, as a species, always had a strong hunch that paradise must exist and one or two settled ideas of what it might be like when we get there: warm, dotted with palm trees, rich in succulent fruits, teeming with docile animals and inhabited by a few highly welcoming and kindly people. Medieval writers summoned the place in their imaginations, Renaissance painters depicted it in their art – and by the 16th century, sailors began to head out across the oceans to find it in reality. It was at points variously identified with the coastline of Panama, the smaller Windward Islands and the north of Madagascar, but the eventual conclusion was that if paradise was located anywhere on Earth, it had to be on a large piece of basalt rock sticking out of the South Pacific 5,700 kilometres east of Australia, originally known as Otaheite and now commonly referred to as Tahiti.

When Louis-Antoine de Bougainville, the first Frenchman to navigate the globe and explore the island, arrived with his two ships on the north-eastern coast at Hitiaa O Te Ra on 2nd April 1768, he was in no doubt as to what he had found. He described a peaceable people living on a diet of tropical fruits and fish in immaculate thatched villages near the beaches. They dressed in grass skirts and seashell necklaces, worshipped nature and the sky, were loving, athletic and graceful, and seemed to know no fear or bitterness. They had never read a book or done mathematics but seemed none the poorer for it. After ten idyllic days, Bougainville renamed the place New Cythera, after the Greek island that had in mythology been home to Aphrodite, goddess of love. In 1788, when a British expedition spent five months exploring the fruit trees of Tahiti, it was not altogether surprising that some of the sailors opted to mutiny from their ship, HMS *Bounty*, rather than head back up to the English Channel. Stories of Tahiti's natural majesty filtered back to Europe and inflamed public imagination. Despite Tahiti's lack of wealth and technological sophistication, it put modernity firmly to shame, for its people seemed to know something that had eluded the cleverest minds in Paris and London: how to be content.

So even now we may head to Charles de Gaulle airport, fly twelve hours to LAX, layover for four hours, then take a nine-hour flight to Fa'a'ā International Airport, 15,700 kilometres away. 'Welcome to Paradise', a sign announces – not hubristically – in the corridor after customs. It is Tahiti's glory as well as its curse to have to stand in for a central piece of our imaginations.

There is enough of what Bougainville saw still in existence to ensure that we will feel we have come to the right place – the brightness of the skies on sunny mornings, the succulence of the fruits, the radiance of the flowers, the beauty of the people – now enhanced by the seven pools, five restaurants, steam rooms, yoga centre and thatched cabins of the InterContinental Tahiti Resort & Spa, nestled in a cove by the airport.

Paul Gauguin,
Street in Tahiti, 1891

Nevertheless, melancholy may descend in the tropics when
it starts to rain, when the hotel guests rush in off the beach
with sodden towels and take shelter in the lounge, when the
manager smiles and assures everyone that it will soon pass and
when we sit reading David Sweetman's definitive biography of
Paul Gauguin (who came in 1891 and gave everyone syphilis),
or Hilary Spurling's biography of Henri Matisse (who came in
1930 and got bored and sad in his room in the now demolished

Hôtel Stuart, a concrete block overlooking the waterfront in the capital, Papeete).

Gauguin ascribed all the island's difficulties to the influence of early 19th-century missionaries. They had made everyone sour; they had led the Tahitians to feel guilty about sex; they had encouraged the women to cover their breasts; they had made the children sing hymns.

Matisse couldn't make sense of his mood. He lacked for nothing. He went for walks by the beach. He tried out a canoe. Yet he felt inadequate to such splendour. His difficult life hitherto hadn't prepared him for such felicity. What was he to do in paradise? He certainly couldn't turn it into art. It was like trying to stare at the sun. He made a few desultory attempts to sketch some flowers on his balcony and some trees by a lagoon, but he was quickly overwhelmed. Only much later, after he had returned to Europe, after a great deal more suffering had descended on him, after the Second World War, after he had developed duodenal cancer and lost the ability to walk, did the lost beauty start to haunt him: the turquoise sea, the madrepores, the Polynesian ground doves, the manta rays and giant turtles. Paradise could be allowed into the imagination only as a subject of longing, finding eventual form in an abstract precis of happiness finished shortly before his death that he called *Memory of Oceania*.

Paradise may simply not suit our nature. We have too much anxiety thrumming through our veins. We get restless, we listen to serpents, we are serpents ourselves, ready to poison and disobey. We bring 'ourselves' to Arcadia; that is, all our fretfulness, regret, dissatisfaction, cluelessness and suppressed

Henri Matisse,
Memory of Oceania, 1952–1953

rage. Those British mutineers ended up killing one another, inciting tribal warfare and, in some cases, going mad. Gauguin tried to slit his throat. It is in paradise that we may feel our inadequacies and melancholy most severely.

Politics
& Melancholy

We're used to dividing how people vote in elections according to the categories of right-wing and left-wing. There might be, however, another, better way of labelling an electorate, which taps into something broader and deeper in human personality. We might apportion people into the camps of Romantic and Melancholic voters. Here is some of what separates these two fundamental electoral types:

Revolution vs. evolution

The Romantic believes that a far better world could be just around the corner, if only bold and swift action could be taken: if we entered an agreement or scrapped an agreement, started a war or ended a war. The Romantic considers a degree of impatience to be a vital resource in governing a nation. They may not think too badly of anger, either. You can be too forgiving, after all. The Romantic is excited by how things might ideally be, and always judges what currently exists in the world by the standard of a better imagined alternative. Most of the time, the current state of things arouses them to intense disappointment as they consider the injustices, prevarications, compromises and timidity of almost everyone in government.

For their part, the Melancholic voter is highly distrustful of sudden gestures and actions. They pay special attention to what can go wrong. They are very concerned to mitigate the downside. They are aware that most things could be a lot worse. Before condemning a policy, they consider the standard of policy across history and may regard a current arrangement as bearable, under the circumstances ... Their view of people is fundamentally dark. They believe that everyone is probably slightly worse than they seem. They feel humans have deeply dangerous impulses, lusts and drives, and believe the task of politics is to try to contain these, rather than to liberate genius, strength, beauty or benevolence. High ideals make them nervous: they are led by a desire not to make anything worse. In so far as they hope for improvement, it is in a cautious, modest way. They dare to suppose that the world may be a marginally better place – in 300 years' time.

Blame vs. responsibility

Romantics see a lot that is wrong with the world and feel confident about analysing who might be to blame for it: perhaps this particular social group or that class ... A problem can't just be no one's fault, and therefore the task of politics is to identify the wrongdoers and respond appropriately. Romantics feel a basic trust in their own capacity for purity. They are sure they would be unable to be as shabby as their enemies, whom they can therefore attack with a clean conscience.

Melancholic voters also notice what is wrong but are highly aware of their own capacity for sinfulness and error, which makes them hesitant about apportioning blame. They recognise how easily they might have been active wrongdoers if circumstances had been different, and suppose that no one has a monopoly on righteousness. They would suggest that evil is pretty proportionately distributed across all groups and classes, and that a priority, therefore, is for us to tolerantly cut each other slack at every turn.

Individuals vs. institutions

Romantic voters believe that everything great in history is the result of talented individuals taking destiny into their hands and struggling against the inertia and conservatism of the mass and, most importantly, of institutions.

Melancholic voters are deeply worried by the possibility of lone actors taking matters into their own hands and, through natural weaknesses which all of us – even the most intelligent – are afflicted by, creating disaster. They are, therefore, on the side of legally grounded, extremely slow-moving institutions that are designed to restrain individual power and contain the capacity of any one person to shift the direction of the group too quickly.

Rightness vs. scepticism

Romantic voters believe it is possible to understand a situation or issue so clearly that one can be sure of complete justice and rightness. Therefore, those who don't agree don't have to be listened to politely. They are evidently wrong – and can be silenced or sidelined as required.

Melancholic voters are extremely alert to the possibility of error in their own and others' analyses of policy. They are, therefore, committed to hearing and tolerating dissenting views – in which they suspect a portion of the truth may always be lodged.

Strength vs. modesty

Romantic voters feel that the best way for a nation to be safe in the world is for it to seem prominently 'strong'.

Melancholic voters feel that the best way to be safe in the world is to be thought well of, and will therefore avoid actions that could upset, alarm or confuse neighbours. They're aware of how easily strength arouses the desire of others to be equally strong back. They suspect the best way to proceed might be to train in private for the worst – but extend a hand of friendship at every public turn.

—

Both Romantic and Melancholic political orientations have important truths to impart. Neither is wholly right or wrong. They need to be balanced. And none of us are, in any case, ever simply one or the other. But because a good political landscape requires a judicious balance of both, at this point in history, in many countries, it might be the Melancholic electoral attitude whose distinctive claims and wisdom we need to listen to most intently and which is most ripe for rediscovery.

The Inner Critic
& Melancholy

We almost all have a character inside our minds whom we might call the inner critic. It tends to pay its visits late at night. It waits until we're very tired or physically depleted, and it then starts to whisper vicious and appalling things to us in order to destroy all possibility of peace, self-confidence and self-compassion. It is, at base, convinced that we shouldn't really exist, and it's extremely subtle and inventive about telling us why. It is, in extremis, the inner critic that tells people to go and kill themselves.

Too often, in the face of yet another onslaught by the inner critic, our minds freeze: we simply don't know how to answer back. We're in a tunnel alone with the critic and forget that there might be any other perspectives to bring to bear on our situation. We let ourselves be assailed by merciless accusations, and sink into self-flagellation and despair.

We should – when our minds clear – prepare one or two things we might say in reply to the critic when it next comes calling.

—

'You're a total loser'

There is never one story of a life. The difference between hope and despair hangs on a different way of telling contrasting stories from the same set of facts. Of course you could spin everything as a tragedy; of course there's enough material for a suicide. But let's try another route. This is another way of telling your life story: 'Against enormous odds, you attempted to live decently; you made some serious errors, as all humans will, and you paid a very heavy price for them. In many ways, you suffered far more than is your due. You've been through hell. Nevertheless, you tried to be good and loved a few people properly and attempted to keep going.' On your gravestone, it might say: 'Tried very hard'. Or: 'Despite everything, heart was in the right place'. And that would be a far kinder and equally valid way to narrate a life.

'You're disgusting, and you definitely don't deserve compassion'

One might at this point wonder where this inner critic comes from. There's only one answer: an inner critic was always an outer critic who has been internalised. You're speaking to yourself as someone else once spoke to you, or once made you feel. Stand back from this deranged, cruel lunatic and question what they are doing in your mind. Is that really a way to speak to anyone? You're happy to acknowledge your failings, all of them, every single one; you're happy to say sorry and atone and make enormous amends and accept what you have coming to you – but this? Does anyone deserve this? This critic just wants you to die – and they don't have a right to walk unhindered, sledgehammer in hand, into the rooms of your mind.

'Everyone else knows how to live apart from you'

Another characteristically harrowing suggestion. In fact, we don't know about others. We only know people from the outside, from what they decide to tell us, and naturally they hide all the bad bits that we're only too aware of in ourselves. Almost certainly, others are going out of their minds and are racked by guilt and fear. Naturally, a few people appear to have perfect lives, but that's only because you don't know them well enough. No one is normal or very happy from close up. Life is a struggle for everyone. Stop comparing what you know of your deep self with the advertising hoardings others have put up about their lives.

'You've made unforgivable mistakes'

That one again. There's no point denying it. The best defence is retreat: of course! Of course you've made some terrible and even some catastrophic mistakes! Of course you've been an idiot! But can you take a moment to remember your childhood, to summon up what you went through, the background you came from? What chance did you have of being even partially sane? It's amazing you're able to stand up and say your own name. We don't do perfect people around here. This is a clinic for the broken. Stop torturing yourself with an idea that you might ever have been perfect; be amazed you exist.

'It's never ever going to get better'

The truth is: you don't know. No one knows the future. The strangest, most awful things have happened very suddenly; and the strangest, loveliest things could happen all of a sudden as well. Despair presumes you know the rest of the story. Keep going.

'Disaster is on the way; a catastrophe is coming'

The inner critic loves to whip up terror; it keeps insisting that something appalling is about to arrive. You should beat this sadistic critic at their own game. Stop hoping that things are going to be fun and then allowing yourself to be scared of potential disaster. Pre-empt the attack. Yes, there may be problems, but in the end, so what? They can be dealt with. Life can go on even at a very reduced rate. People have been able to keep going with only one leg, or in exile, or down to one friend or a pittance. It can be handled.

'No one loves you or could ever love you'

That one sounds especially tempting, particularly around three in the morning. Yet it can't be the truth. You've suffered, and you're honest and you can be kind. That's enough for someone to stick with you. Most humans love winners, but you don't need 'most' humans. Concentrate on the small subset with very big hearts. Be honest with them about your pain; they'll find their way to you.

'You're so ugly'

Yes, possibly, but so are lots of people and when you love them, you start to see their soul and you love their character. You probably haven't thought much about what most of the people you deeply love look like in a long time.

'Where will you be in five years?'

At this point, who cares? Cut life up into far smaller increments. See if you can make it to the next meal and a nice bath, and that would be achievement enough. Reduce ambition as a precondition of survival. Count it as a triumph if nothing absolutely terrible happens in the next hour. Celebrate the peaceful next ten minutes.

'You want to die, don't you? And you probably should'

Absolutely not. You're just finding it hard to live, but you want to live very much. You want to find a way to be a decent human and to keep going. And you will.

—

At which point, the inner critic might walk off in a fury at being resisted and for a few hours leave us alone. In the meantime, we should remember what it felt like to be five years old and looked after tenderly by someone who stroked our hair and had a kind nickname for us. Things have become harder for us since then, but what we deserve hasn't changed: all of us are still small children, worthy of forgiveness and in need of a lot of slack. We're muddling through and trying to do our very best in the circumstances. We can be melancholic; we can resist tragedy.

Gardening
& Melancholy

It is crucial to note the subtitle of 18th-century Europe's most famous novel, written in three inspired days in 1759: *Candide*, or *Optimism*. If there was one central target that its author wanted satirically to destroy, it was the hope of his age, a hope that centred around science, love, technical progress and reason. Voltaire was enraged. Of course science wasn't going to improve the world; it would merely give new power to tyrants. Of course philosophy would not be able to explain away the problem of evil; it would only show up our vanity. Of course love was an illusion, power a chimera, humans irredeemably wicked and the future absurd. Of all this, his readers were to be left in no doubt. Hope was a disease and it was Voltaire's generous goal to try to cure us of it.

Nevertheless, Voltaire's novel is not simply a tragic tale, nor is his own philosophy mordantly nihilistic. The book ends on a memorably tender and stoic note; the tone is elegiac; we encounter one of the finest expressions of the melancholic viewpoint ever written. Candide and his companions have travelled the world and suffered immensely: they have known persecution, shipwrecks, rapes, earthquakes, smallpox, starvation and torture. They have – more or less – survived and, in the final pages, find themselves in Turkey (a country Voltaire especially admired), living on a small farm in a suburb of Istanbul. One day they learn of trouble at the Ottoman court: two viziers and the mufti have been strangled and several of their associates impaled. The news causes upset and fear in many. Near their farm, Candide, walking with his friends Martin and Pangloss, passes an old man who is peacefully and indifferently sitting under an orange bower next to his house:

> Pangloss, who was as inquisitive as he was argumentative, asked the old man what the name of the strangled Mufti was. 'I don't know,' answered the worthy man, 'and I have never known the name of any Mufti, nor of any Vizier. I have no idea what you're talking about; my general view is that people who meddle with politics usually meet a miserable end, and indeed they deserve to. I never bother with what is going on in Constantinople; I only worry about sending the fruits of the garden which I cultivate off to be sold there.' Having said these words, he invited the strangers into his house; his two sons and two daughters presented them with several sorts of sherbet, which they had made themselves, with kaimak enriched with the candied-peel of citrons, with oranges, lemons, pine-apples, pistachio-nuts, and Mocha coffee … after which the two daughters of the honest Muslim perfumed the strangers' beards. 'You must have a vast and magnificent estate,' said Candide to the Turk. 'I have only twenty acres,' replied the old man; 'I and my children cultivate them; and our labour preserves us from three great evils: weariness, vice, and want.' Candide, on his

way home, reflected deeply on what the old man had said. 'This honest Turk,' he said to Pangloss and Martin, 'seems to be in a far better place than kings … I also know,' said Candide, 'that we must cultivate our garden.'

Voltaire, who liked to stir the prejudices of his largely Christian readers, especially enjoyed giving the idea for the most important line in his book – and arguably the most important adage in modern thought – to a Muslim, the true philosopher of the book known only as 'the Turk': *Il faut cultiver notre jardin*. 'We must cultivate our garden', or, as it has variously been translated, 'we must grow our vegetables', 'we must tend to our lands' or 'we need to work our fields'.

What did Voltaire mean by his gardening advice? That we must keep a good distance between ourselves and the world, because taking too close an interest in politics or public opinion is a fast route to aggravation and danger. We should know well enough at this point that humans are troublesome and will never achieve – at a state level – anything like the degree of logic and goodness we would wish for. We should never tie our personal moods to the condition of a whole nation or people in general, or we would need to weep continuously. We need to live in our own small plots, not the heads of strangers. At the same time, because our minds are haunted and prey to anxiety and despair, we need to keep ourselves busy. We need a project. It shouldn't be too large or dependent on many other people. The project should send us to sleep every night weary but satisfied. It could be bringing up a child, writing a book, looking after a house, running a small shop or managing a little business. Or, of course, tending to a few acres. Note Voltaire's geographical modesty. We should give up on trying to cultivate the whole of humanity; we should give up on things at a national or international scale. Take just a few acres and make those your focus. Take a small orchard and grow lemons and apricots. Take some beds and grow asparagus and carrots. Stop worrying yourself with humanity if you ever want peace of mind again. Who cares what's happening in Constantinople or what's up with the grand mufti? Live quietly like the old Turk, enjoying the sunshine in the orange bower next to your house. This is Voltaire's stirring, ever-relevant form of horticultural quietism. We have been warned – and guided.

It is no coincidence that Voltaire put his lines about the cultivation of the garden into the mouth of a Muslim. He had done a lot of reading about Islam for his *Essay on Universal History*, published three years before, and properly understood the role of gardens in its theology. For Muslims, because the world at large can never be rendered perfect, it is the task of the pious to try to give a foretaste of what should ideally be by creating a well-tended garden (and where that is not possible, a depiction of a garden in a rug). There should be four canals that allude to the four rivers of paradise in which are said to flow water, milk, wine and honey, and where they intersect represents the *umbilicus mundi*, the navel of the world, where the gift of life emerged. Gardening is no trivial pastime. It's a central way of shielding ourselves from the influence of the chaotic, dangerous world beyond, while focusing our energies on something that can reflect the goodness and grace we long for.

Melancholics know that humans – ourselves foremost among them – are beyond redemption. We melancholics have given up on dreams of complete purity and unblemished happiness.

Bishndas, illustration from the *Baburnama*
showing the Mughal emperor Babur
supervising the laying out of a Kabul
garden, c. 1590

We know that this world is, for the most part, hellish and heartbreakingly vicious. We know that our minds are full of demons that will not leave us alone for long. Nevertheless, we are committed to not slipping into despondency. We remain deeply interested in kindness, in friendship, in art, in family life – and in spending some very quiet local afternoons gardening. The melancholic position is ultimately the only sensible one for a broken human. It's where one gets to after one has been hopeful, after one has tried love, after one has been tempted by fame, after one has despaired, after one has gone mad, after one has considered ending it – and after one has decided conclusively to keep going. It captures the best possible attitude to pain, and the wisest orientation of a weary mind towards what remains hopeful and good.

Image credits

p. 10t   Nicholas Hilliard, *Young Man Among Roses*, c. 1585–1595. Vellum and watercolour, 13 cm × 3 cm. Victoria and Albert Museum, London, England / Wikimedia Commons

p. 10b   Isaac Oliver, *Edward Herbert, 1st Baron Herbert of Cherbury*, 1613–1614. Watercolour on vellum, 18.1 cm × 22.9 cm. Powis Castle, Welshpool, Wales. National Trust / Wikimedia Commons

p. 13   Albrecht Dürer, *Melencolia I*, 1514. Engraving, 24.5 cm × 19.2 cm. National Gallery of Art, Washington, D.C., USA. Gift of R. Horace Gallatin. Image courtesy National Gallery of Art.

p. 17   Zacharias Dolendo, *Saturn as Melancholy*, 1595. Rijksmuseum.

p. 36t   Workshop of Giovanni Bellini, *Madonna and Child*, c. 1510. Oil on wood, 34.3 cm × 27.6 cm. The Metropolitan Museum of Art, New York, USA. The Jules Bache Collection, 1949. Image courtesy The Metropolitan Museum of Art.

p. 36b   Sandro Botticelli, *Madonna and Child*, c. 1470. Tempera on panel, 74 cm × 54 cm. National Gallery of Art, Washington, D.C., USA. Andrew W. Mellon Collection. Image courtesy National Gallery of Art.

p. 40   NASA / JHUAPL / SWRI

p. 91   Rainer Ebert / Wikimedia Commons

p. 92   Paul Kozlowski + © F.L.C. / ADAGP, Paris and DACS, London 2021

p. 93   Luis García / Wikimedia Commons

p. 112   Agnes Martin, *Morning*, 1965. Acrylic paint and graphite on canvas. 182.6 cm × 181.9 cm. Tate Museum, London, England. © Photo: Tate © Agnes Martin Foundation, New York / DACS 2021

p. 115   Agnes Martin Gallery, Harwood Museum of Art, Taos, NM. © Agnes Martin Foundation, New York / DACS 2021. Photo: Courtesy Rick Romancito / The Taos News

p. 117   Agnes Martin, *I love the Whole World*, 1993. Acrylic paint and graphite on canvas, 152.4 cm × 152.4 cm. Private Collection, London. © Agnes Martin Foundation, New York / DACS 2021

p. 122   Katsushika Hokusai, *Ejiri in Suruga Province (Sunshū Ejiri)*, 10th
          image from the series *Thirty-six Views of Mount Fuji (Fugaku
          sanjūrokkei)*, c. 1830–1832. Woodblock print; ink and
          color on paper, 25.1 cm × 37.5 cm. The Metropolitan Museum
          of Art, New York, USA. Henry L. Phillips Collection, Bequest
          of Henry L. Phillips, 1939. Image courtesy The Metropolitan
          Museum of Art.

p. 125   Katsushika Hokusai, *The Inume Pass in Kai Province (Kōshū Inume
          tōge)*, 8th image from the series *Thirty-six Views of Mount Fuji
          (Fugaku sanjūrokkei)*, c. 1831–1832. Woodblock print;
          ink and colour on paper, 25.1 cm × 37.8 cm. Credit as above.

p. 126   Katsushika Hokusai, *Under the Wave off Kanagawa (Kanagawa oki
          nami ura)* or *The Great Wave*, 1st image from the series *Thirty-six
          Views of Mount Fuji (Fugaku sanjūrokkei)*, c. 1830–1832. Woodblock
          print; ink and colour on paper, 25.7 cm × 37.9 cm. Credit as
          above.

p. 143t   Robert Landau / Alamy

p. 143b   Andre Jenny / Alamy

p. 145t   FLHC11 / Alamy

p. 145b   Thomson200 / Wikimedia Commons

p. 150   Jan Brueghel (the Younger), *Paradise*, c. 1650. Oil on oak wood,
          60 cm × 42.4 cm. Gemäldegalerie museum, Berlin, Germany.
          Universal Images Group North America LLC / Alamy

p. 153   Paul Gauguin, *Street in Tahiti*, 1891. Oil on canvas, 115.5 cm x
          88.5 cm. Toledo Museum of Art, Toledo, USA / Wikimedia
          Commons

p. 155   Henri Matisse, *Memory of Oceania*, 1952–1953. Gouache on
          paper, cut and pasted, and charcoal on paper mounted on
          canvas, 284.4 cm x 286.4 cm. © Succession H. Matisse / DACS
          2021. Photo: © Scala

p. 171   Bishndas, illustration from the *Baburnama* showing the
          Mughal emperor Babur supervising the laying out of a Kabul
          garden, c. 1590. Watercolour on paper, 21.7 cm x 14.3 cm.
          Victoria and Albert Museum, London, England / Wikimedia
          Commons

The School of Life is a global organisation helping people lead more fulfilled lives. It is a resource for helping us understand ourselves, for improving our relationships, our careers and our social lives – as well as for helping us find calm and get more out of our leisure hours. We do this through films, workshops, books, apps, gifts and community. You can find us online, in stores and in welcoming spaces around the globe.

THESCHOOLOFLIFE.COM